The Harlem Book of the Dead

The HARLEM BOOK of the DEAD

James Van Der Zee • Owen Dodson
Camille Billops

with a Foreword by Toni Morrison

PRIMARY INFORMATION

To Gaynella

J.V.D.Z.

To Edith, Lillian, and Kenneth,
my sisters and brother

O.D.

To my family: James Hatch, Alma and Walter Dotson, Bill Billops, Billie, Michael, Suzanne, Camille, and Jan Browning, Josephine and George Harvey, Josie Dotson, Carol Penn, and Judy Glover.

To my friends: Leo Hamalian, Roz Myers, Ruth Sherman and The Friends of Van Der Zee, Donna Mussenden, and Jeanie Black.

C.B.

Foreword

It is fashionable these days to hear among photography lovers the cry, "Oh, those early photographers really knew how to take pictures." Part of the enthusiasm is not critical evaluation but simple nostalgia: a love affair with the past made more loving because the beloved is no longer with us and able to assert itself. Part of it is simple weariness—weariness of contemporary photojournalism that comes pouring into our living rooms via newspapers, magazines, television and film documentaries.

When we look at the work of James Van Der Zee, however, the statement is neither sentimental nor reactionary. His photography is truly rare—*sui generis.* What is so clear in his pictures and so marked in his words is the passion and the vision, not of the camera but of the photographer. The narrative quality, the intimacy, the humanity of his photographs are stunning, and the proof, if any is needed, is in this collection of pictures devoted exclusively to the dead about which one can only say, "How living are his portraits of the dead." So living, so "undead," that the prestigious writer, Owen Dodson, is stirred to poetry in which life trembles in every metaphor.

That this remarkable concert of Black subject, Black poet, Black photographer and Black artist focuses on the dead is significant for it is true what Africans say: "The Ancestor lives as long as there are those who remember." THE HARLEM BOOK OF THE DEAD, conceived and nurtured by Camille Billops, cherishes that remembrance and enlightens us as only memory can.

Toni Morrison

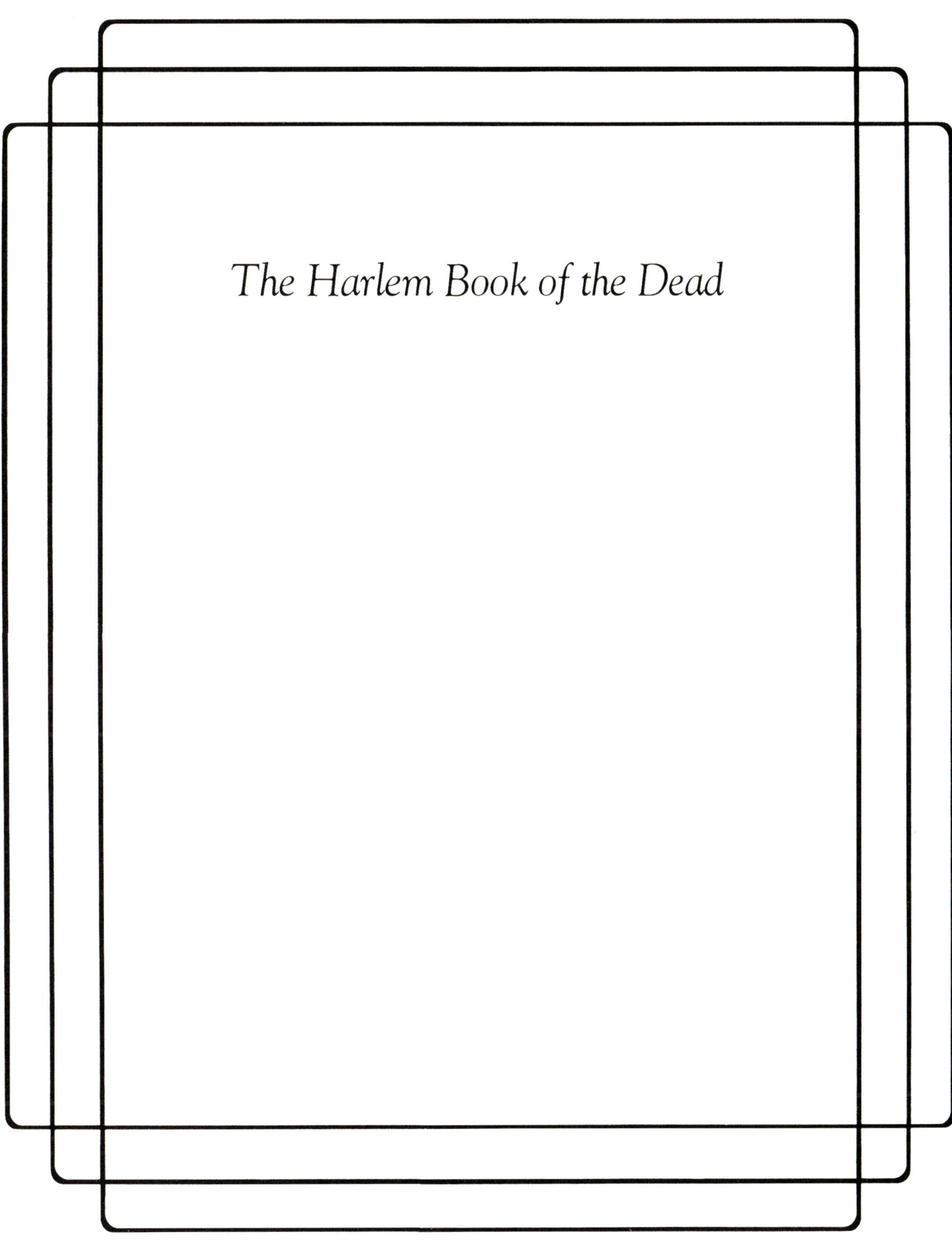

The Harlem Book of the Dead

Introduction

The Harlem rituals of death have parallels with those of the ancient necropolis of Egypt. They are in the continuum of those on the Nile of four thousand years ago. Today, a kindly God the Father, Son, and Holy Ghost, or newly arrived Allah, have replaced Osiris, god of the underworld; the *Bible* with its chants and songs has replaced the old texts of the *Book of the Dead.*

Death is the moment called quittin' time, when we freeze in place like tomb figures or ancient wall paintings or photographs on a mantlepiece in Harlem. Family and friends witness the moment when the preacher sings out the life of the deceased, hoping to distract Satan or Anubis, with his great scale, from weighing the bad deeds against the good.

The morticians in Toppins' or Micky's South Carolina funeral parlors, with no memory of Thebes, still prepare pots of paint to decorate the dead for the afterlife. Shabby viewing rooms become mock burial chambers for king- and queen-size tucked satin coffins. Everything that is needed for the journey has been accounted for: flowers, "best" clothes, friends, songs, farewells, and, for the dead children, never-slept-in cribs, empty baby bottles, toys and ribbons. At the curb waits the great hearse to bear the dead to the final resting place; granite tombstones mark the entrance to paradise or to hell. At the grave, the living bless the gound in the name of Ol' Death or The Grim Reaper in the hope of eternal life, come their turn.

Death, creator and destroyer: Death is a livelihood for the gravedigger, a veil of tears and pain for the widowed. This book presents two of Death's oldest companions—the portrait artist and the poet, both long represented upon the ancient walls of tombs. Photographing the dead was a living for James Van Der Zee; he speaks of the lighting, his camera, the relatives, the practical side of life. Owen Dodson speaks of life, too, but as a poet who, by means of a double vision, looks into the mind and heart of the dead, where he sees the soul before its God. Mr. Van Der Zee helps the undertaker wash the body; Mr. Dodson helps the priest cleanse the soul.

Two ancient views, two truths, two ways of loving humankind.

Camille Billops Hatch-Billops Collection

A Very Long Conversation with James Van Der Zee at the Age of Ninety-One

JAMES VAN DER ZEE: I say, "Why should a spirited mortal feel proud, when like a swift, fleet meteor or fast-flying cloud, man passes through life to his rest in the grave?" They've asked me, "How do I feel?" I told them that there's nothing to it; you do things the way they ought to be done. I don't see anything to be proud about. It's pretty difficult for a man to feel proud when knowing as he does the short space of time he's here and all paths, even those of our greatest glory, lead but to the grave. So it is very difficult to feel proud when Death says this. You're here today and gone sometimes today.

CAMILLE BILLOPS: I GUESS WE'VE BEGUN THIS VERY LONG CONVERSATION, HAVEN'T WE?

JAMES VAN DER ZEE: Yes, I guess we have.

DO YOU KNOW MUCH ABOUT THE HISTORY OF TAKING PICTURES OF DEAD PEOPLE? DID THEY DO THIS KIND OF PHOTOGRAPHY DURING THE TIME OF THE DAGUERREOTYPE?

Undoubtedly they did. They probably photographed every aspect of life during that time and before that, there was the portrait painters who used to paint pictures of the deceased. Sometimes it took a long time, transportation being what it was, for them to get there. The relatives would have to try and preserve the deceased until the painter arrived. This was a long time ago and they didn't have embalming in those days.

I've gotten pictures from the West Indies, that they'd taken there, where they had them in the casket, kind of standing up. The pictures were sent here to me to recopy. I'd recopy them and probably put some of these Biblical figures around them and make the picture look a little more like the ones that I had taken. One day, when I was down in my studio on Seventh Avenue, a woman come from the Hotel Theresa and said, "When my brother died, my mother and father paid over fifty dollars for funeral pictures, and they wasn't near as good as these that you have here."

WHAT DID YOU CHARGE FOR YOUR FUNERAL PICTURES?

I would get thirty-five dollars for a photograph, which was good money in those days.

WERE YOUR CLIENTS WEALTHY?

I don't think that they would be called wealthy like you might think of today, but they could afford to pay for the pictures. Harlem wasn't like it is today.

WERE YOUR FUNERAL PICTURES THE ONLY PHOTOGRAPHS THAT YOU DID OF THE DEAD?

Occasionally I did some autopsy pictures, but not many. The relatives of the deceased would request it when autopsies had been performed without their consent. It seemed to be for legal purposes; but I don't know any more than that. During the whole time I never took more than five or six of those pictures.

WERE ALL YOUR FUNERAL PICTURES TAKEN IN THE FUNERAL PARLOR OR WERE SOME OF THEM TAKEN IN THE HOME?

They were taken in the funeral parlors. I went there just before they were getting ready to take the casket out.

DID YOU EVER ATTEND ANY OF THESE FUNERALS?

I never was at the funerals where I took pictures, never knew the people. The relatives all used different ministers that said different things. I do remember Rev. Monroe. Everybody used to try to get him 'cause he specialized in funerals. He would just call them (the dead), "Sit up, John! John, these are your people."

WHY DID YOU PUT INSERTS INTO YOUR PHOTOGRAPHS?

Well, I just put them in to take away the gruesomeness of the picture, to make it look more like "suffering little children to come unto me and I'll give you rest." In some cases I put in biblical scriptures.

WHO WAS THE FIRST PERSON YOU PHOTOGRAPHED IN A COFFIN?

I don't know who that could have been; I would have to think back. I took some of my first pictures around 1920 or so. I'm trying to think of what camera I used for them. I took the big 8x10 camera with me; it wasn't as heavy then as it is today. Things have a way of getting heavier as the years go by.

I HAVE HEARD SOME CASES WHERE PEOPLE WHO HAD THE FUNERAL SERVICE AT HOME WOULD HAVE THE ICEMAN COME AND PUT ICE UNDER THE DECEASED ON A SPECIAL RACK. HAVE YOU EVER RUN ACROSS THIS?

No, I can't say that I did. All my pictures, as I said, were done in the funeral parlor and they didn't do anything like that. I do, however, remember my grandfather, David Osterhout, who was a gravedigger in Lenox, Massachusetts, telling me stories of how he used to have to move some of the coffins from one place to another. Sometimes the families of the deceased would have the bodies moved to the family plot. He said that he had found some of them turned over in the caskets or be in different positions when they opened up the casket. During that time they didn't embalm people, so maybe some of them weren't dead when they were put in the casket. Of course there were the stories of the dead people's hair and fingernails growing after death.

One time I dreamed I went to make a picture of a dead woman who reached in her chest and took out her heart and threw it over here, then she reached in there and took out something else and threw it over there. I just waited to see if she was going to take out something else... but I wasn't scared or nothing like that in the dream.

Death always happens
To somebody else,
Not the dead.

Somebody—friends,
Somebody—aunts,
Cousins, nephews, mothers,
Fathers, sisters, brothers—
Not the dead.

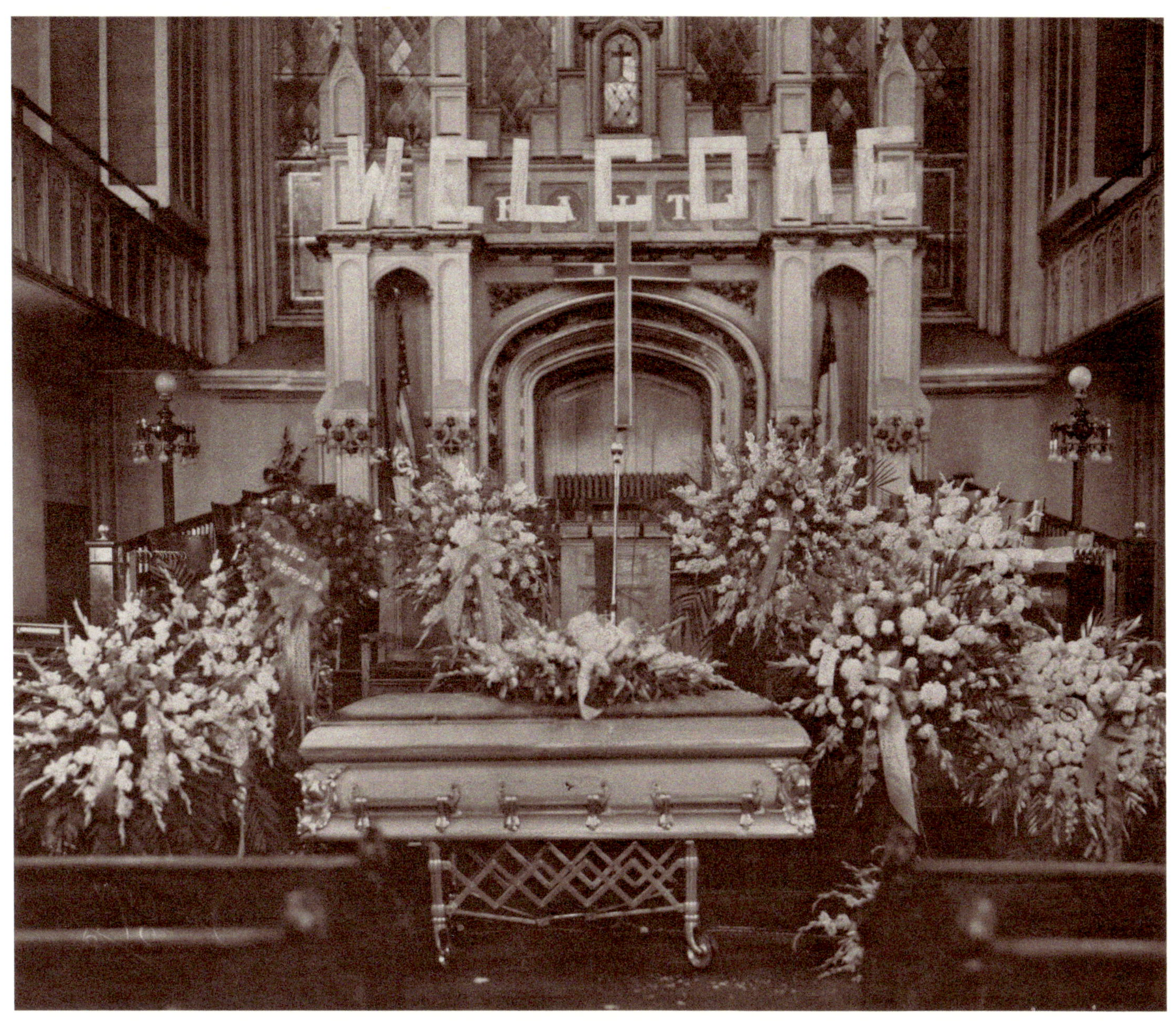
WELCOME

The dead are the signs
Of our cross;
The bury-hour:
Our living crucifixion.

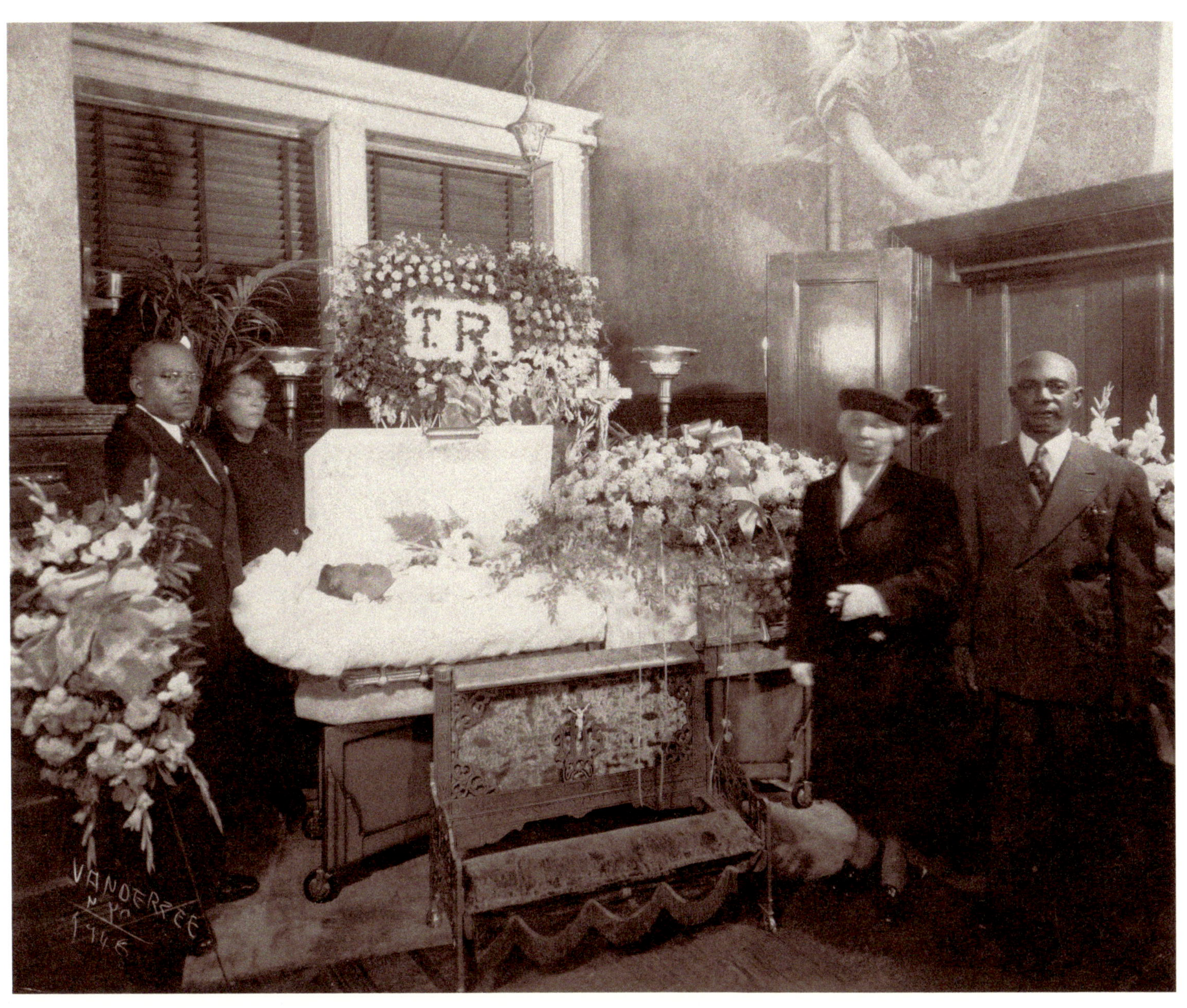
T.R.
VANDERZEE
N.Y.
1946

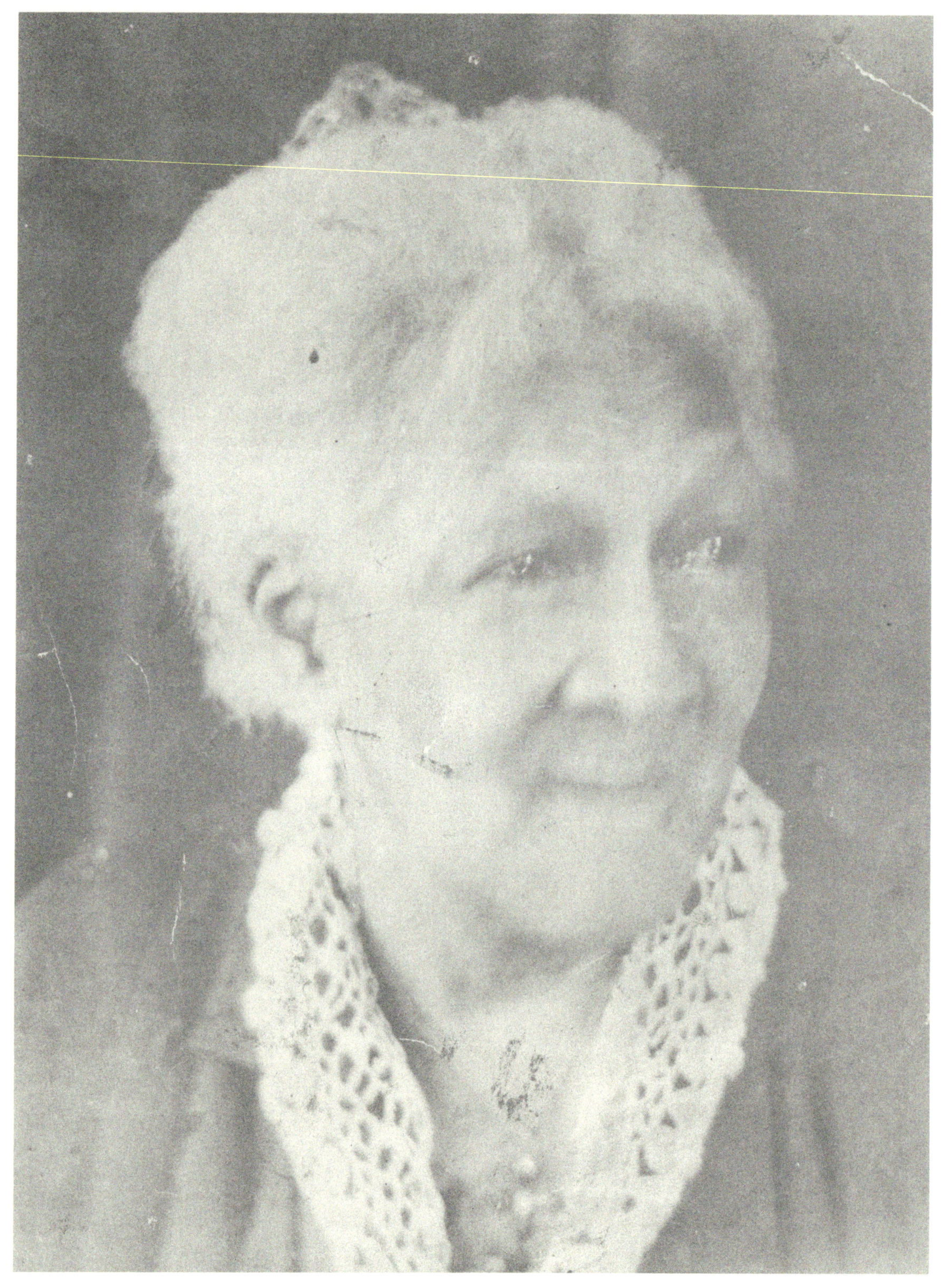

Mothers & Prophesies

My mother used to always stand at the foot of the bed and tell me about how some of the women would trick me and find I was a substantial, steady-working fellow, but I figured that couldn't happen to me.

WELL, DO YOU FEEL THAT YOU HAVE BEEN TRICKED?

No, I don't think so.

MANY MEN FEEL THAT WAY, MR. VAN DER ZEE. DID YOUR MOTHER TEACH YOU THAT WOMEN TRICKED MEN?

Well, now, she put that idea in my head. Why, that was up in Massachusetts; I didn't see how anything like that was goin' to happen up there because of chances, in a way of speaking. But she prepared me, I guess, for the future events.

WHAT ELSE DID YOUR MOTHER TEACH YOU?

Well, she taught me how to be polite and God-fearing and courteous and eloquent, and many of the things that are essential in life. She never had too much trouble with us kids.

HOW DID YOUR MOTHER FEEL ABOUT YOUR FIRST CHILD BEING CONCEIVED OUT OF WEDLOCK?

She accepted it. They all seemed to have accepted it gracefully. It wasn't dreadfully early. I was glad of that because when we were beginning to get ready for the birth I said, "Well, it'd be the best way for me to go home." She was gettin' kind of big and so in the spring of the year, why we headed home to Lenox, Massachusetts.

WHY DID YOU HEAD FOR HOME? WAS THAT ALWAYS HOME TO YOU?

That was always home. Yes, that was the place where everything else had happened.

WAS YOUR MOTHER THE ONE WHO TOOK CARE OF EVERYONE?

Yes, she was a very mothering woman. It was a very nice time. We never quarreled together or anything, everything went on peacefully, and I don't remember ever hearing my mother and father having any contentions or arguments. The worst thing I ever heard him say was "confound it." He was a very capable man. He had a father who was a pretty good mechanic and carpenter, who put additions on the back of our buildings and built the fireplace, a bigger billiard room and all those things. Even though Dad was only gettin' six hundred dollars a year we had a garden, cows, horses, and chickens. My aunts were bakers and when we needed bread and cake we just walked into the bakers shop in town and got what we needed. They were very good cooks and bakers. My brother and I would help her distribute the bread and things. They also made pies and all the bread that was used for the Communion in the Episcopal Church for many years. My grandparents had another house which was probably about fifty or seventy-five feet away from ours, the three houses were right along on the road together.

DID YOU OWN THOSE HOUSES?

Yes. They owned those houses. My grandfather, he was sexton of the Congregational Church, which was a big church up on the hill. He also did all the gravedigging. My aunt, who was dead, had these two daughters who had a laundry business there, they also did home laundry.

THEY WERE VERY INDEPENDENT PEOPLE WEREN'T THEY?

Yes they were. One of my aunts lived until she was a hundred and six years old.

HOW LONG DID YOUR MOTHER LIVE?

I think she was about seventy-five when she died. My mother died because she just got tired of living. I photographed her just two hours after she had died in bed.

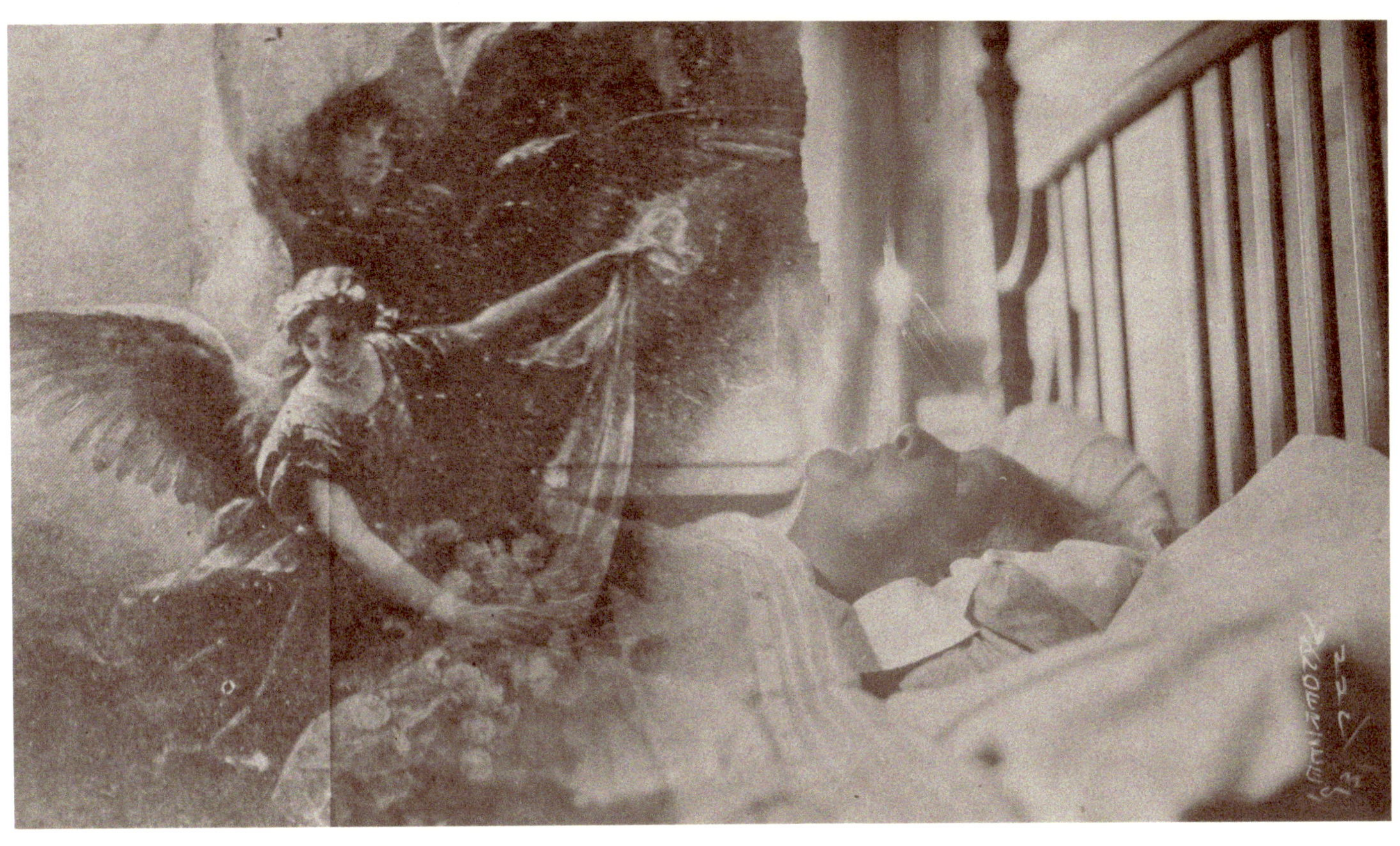

Allegory of Seafaring Black Mothers

How many mothers with their grit,
With their bony and long dreams,
Have dared to splash with us out to sea?
They weighed anchor while we,
While we played marbles or dominoes;
Hide-and-seek games
With biology, spelling, geography;
Then at twilight, crossed-legged, the mothers
Recited all the higher algebra of pride:
Teaching of how to do, what not to do,
With grace toward the chemistry of man.
        Mothers hoping in the dark to God,
        Grunting spells into the decks,
        Then mopping up with elbow grease
        So we could walk safely
        In any season's tantrum.
        Mothers bargaining with
                ancient sins
        To leave us be to learn
                and live and win;
        Mothers milking nanny goats
        To make us strong;
        Telling the fortunes of bees
        For honey to sweeten bile.
In the suburbs of dreams

They dug the earth with their
fingernails,
Planted oaks to shelter us
with acorns for insurance.
Nailed the Government to a cross
For their stingy aid when we
were desolate.
At night they played hymns
on their kazoos,
or whistled spirituals:
the haunted tunes.
Sometimes whales accom-
panied them.
They dived into the waters
(where our ancestors might have died),
Witnessed the intercourse
of mermaids
As they scrubbed the ass
of the ship.
Then lo and behold a
new breed was born.
How many mothers with their grit,
With their bony and long dreams
Have dared to splash with us
out to sea?

She been heated on the anvil
Of life, beaten an' blazed,
Then purity come shaped
For her Savior into this iron black rod.
Oh God, I would've given my gold tooth
An' my right arm...
Oh Savior, this Deaconess
Were in love with the hem
Of Thy garment.

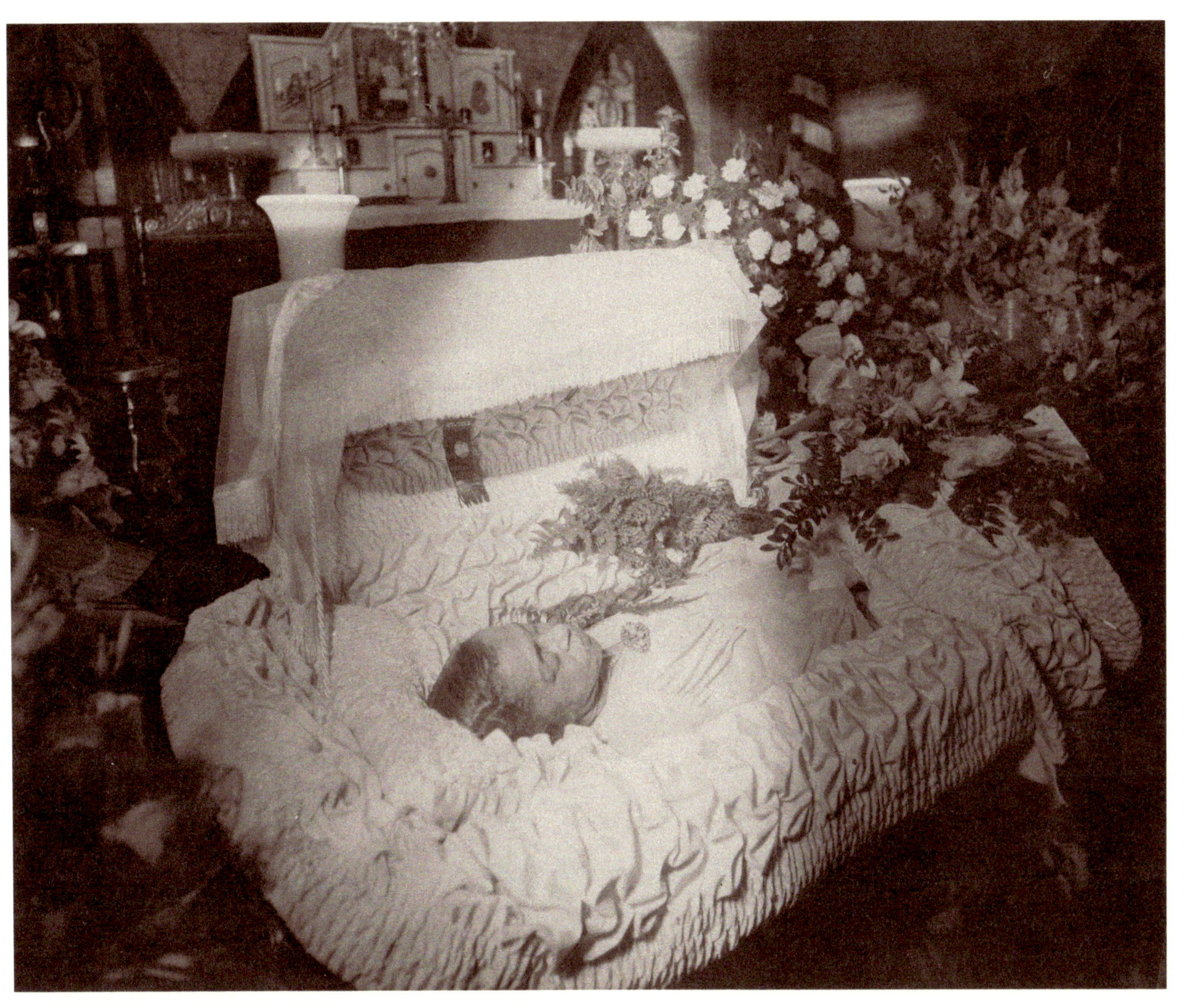

I do not mind the silence.
What I fear is the ground or the fire.
If I could only rent here,
Call my florist
For fresh roses or even dandelions.
The insurance I'd spend on me.
Do this for your mama, son.

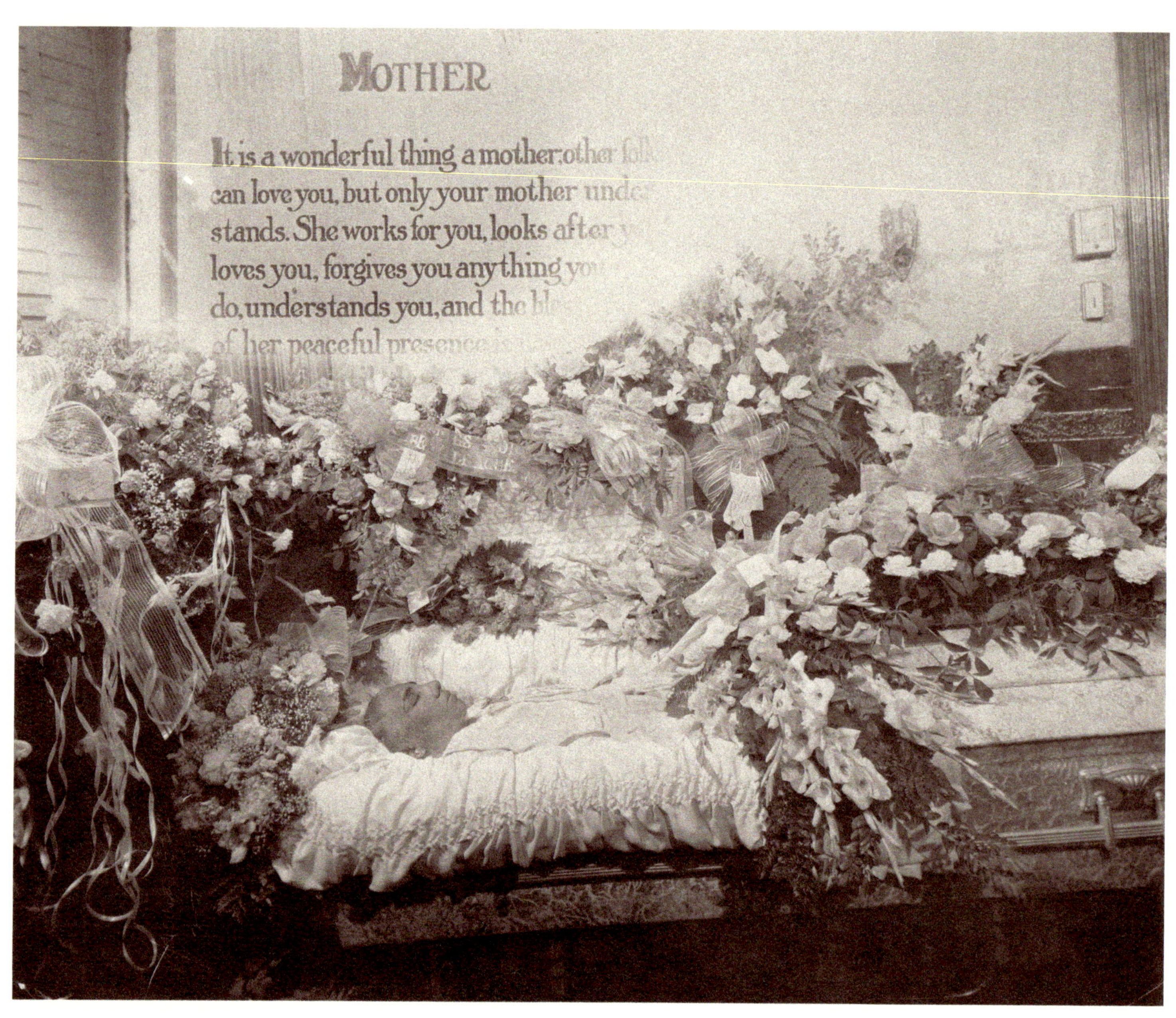

Your ulcers didn't deserve you, dear.

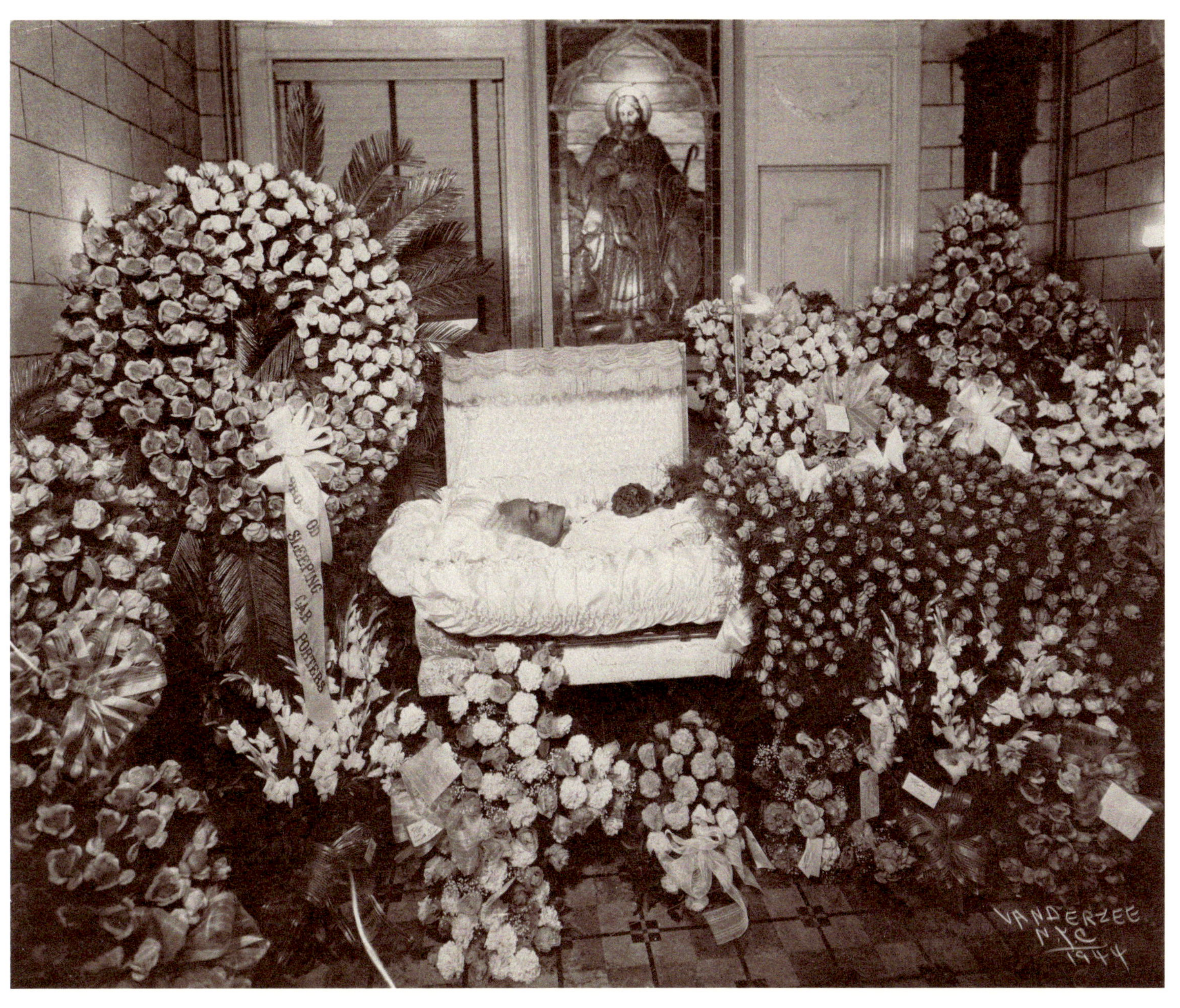

Cease messin' around
And read me the messages
On the tags of my flowers.

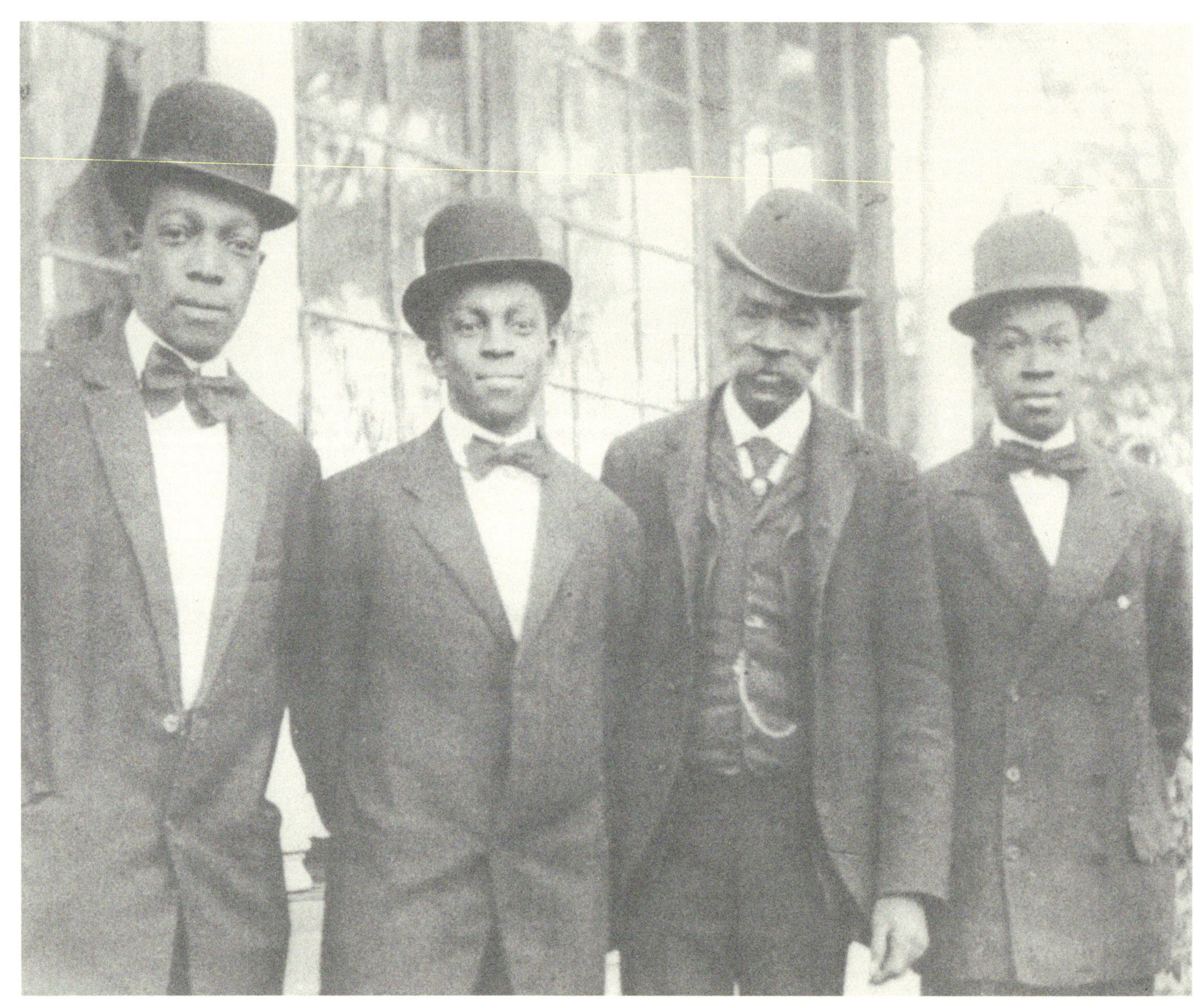

Fathers & the Better People

My father was quite an up-to-date man. He associated with a great many of the better people, and he knew all the answers.

IN THE BOOK *JAMES VAN DER ZEE* [Morgan & Morgan, 1973] THERE'S A PICTURE IN WHICH YOU, YOUR BROTHERS, AND YOUR FATHER ARE WEARING BOWLER HATS. YOU LOOK LIKE A BUNCH OF DANDIES.

Those were just our derby hats. They wore them in those days. In the wintertime, we wore derbys. Of course, you did a lot of shovelin' snow, and that's the time when you'd wear a cap sometimes.

HOW DID YOU SEE YOURSELF AS A YOUNG MAN?

Well, we were all robust and steady because we had to cut down a lot of trees and saw up the wood for the fireplaces and just take care of the gardens and feed the cows and horses. With so much to do all the time, my father needed plenty of help.

WHAT KIND OF PERSON WAS YOUR FATHER?

He was very quiet and humorous. He was a very good butler and waiter and roundabout man. He had, as I said, grown up with the better people, always waited on them and served them, and therefore became a gentleman.

WHAT DO YOU MEAN BY "THE BETTER PEOPLE?"

The aristocrats of that time. Later my father became very ill. He used to take out a lot of ashes, which caused him to get "black lung" or T.B.

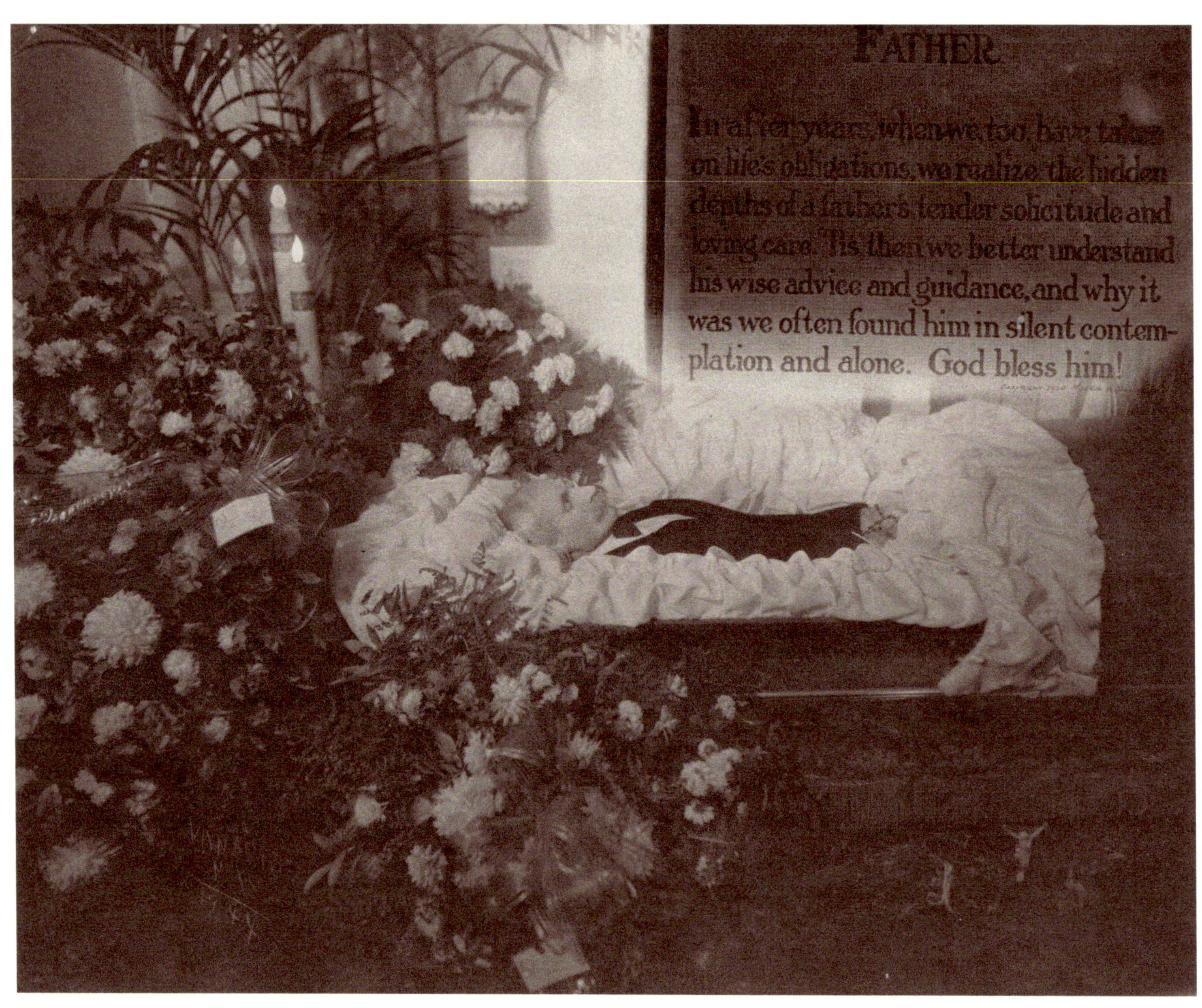
FATHER
In after years, when we, too, have taken
on life's obligations, we realize the hidden
depths of a father's tender solicitude and
loving care. 'Tis, then we better understand
his wise advice and guidance, and why it
was we often found him in silent contem-
plation and alone. God bless him!

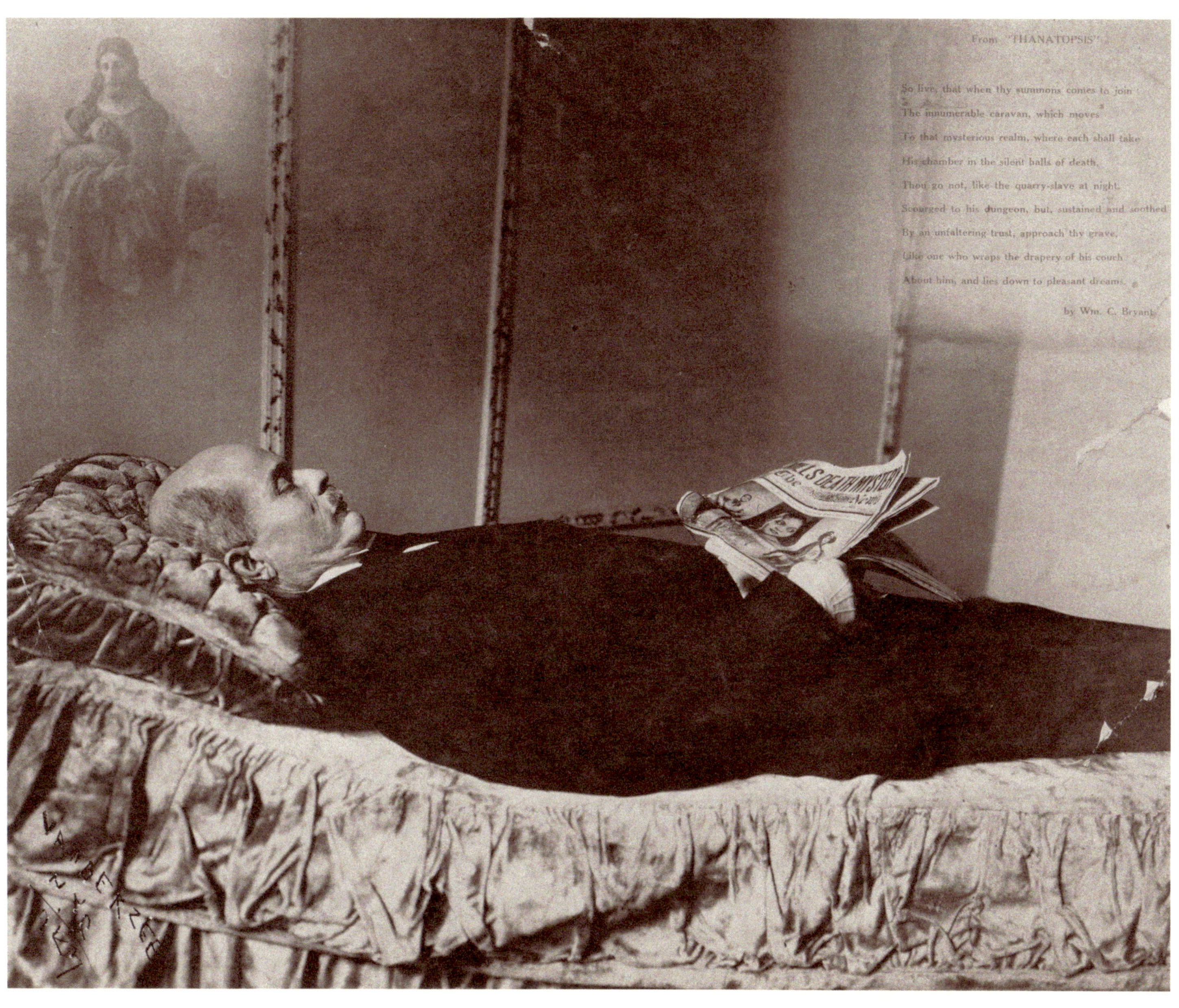

I prayed that on the day I died
Nobody else prominent would be dead
The obituary page was supposed to be all about me today.
Florence Mills, the greatest, died on my day
Look-a-here Lord,
I was a faithful servant
Over many a money year.

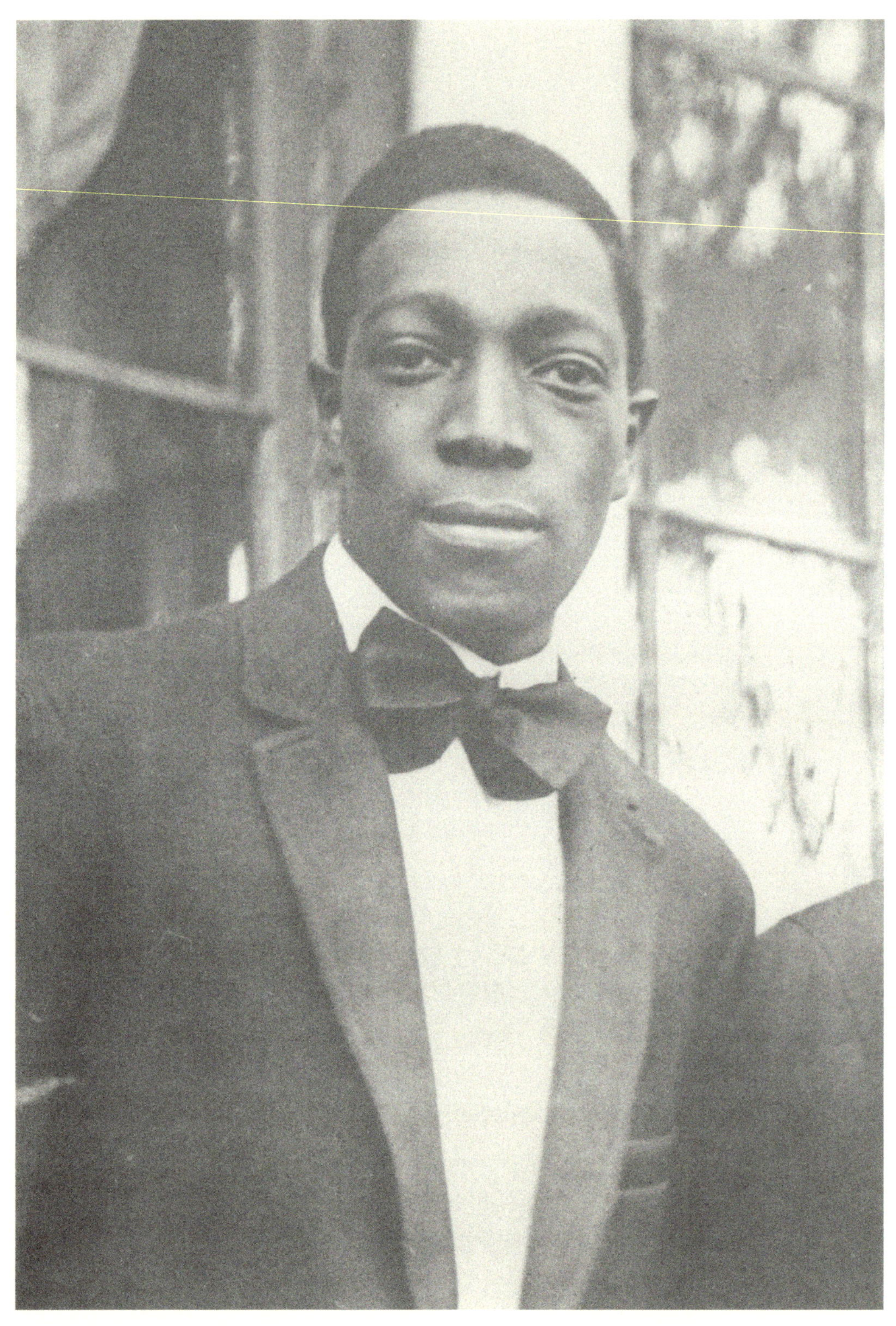

James Van Der Zee, The Young Man

DID YOU RECEIVE FORMAL MUSIC TRAINING WHEN YOU WERE GROWING UP?

In Lenox I had a few lessons on the piano, but mainly I picked it up myself. I did, however, study the violin with Professor Lemare, who gave lessons at the Aspenwald Hotel during the summer months. Later on I studied violin at the Carlton Conservatory of Music on Twenty-Third Street in New York.

AS A YOUNG MAN, WERE YOUR IDEAS OF SUCCESS ABOUT THE SAME AS YOUR FRIENDS'?

No, I didn't think about the marvelous things, or anything special, I just liked music and I mixed with the guys that were interested along that line. At that time I had the Harlem Orchestra, which got started about nineteen-ten or so. According to the different occasions that we played at, we would use from two to six different musicians at a time, which we got from the Amsterdam Musical Association that I belonged to. We would play at the various social events: birthday parties, club dances, dancing schools, and so forth. We even played up in Lenox, Massachusetts, at an affair that the Aspenwald Hotel bellmen and waiters gave at a hall in town.

But as time grew on, why, music became crowded out by the graphophone and the gramophone, which, as I saw, were going to drive the musicians out. I felt that it was necessary for other means of occupation and support. Even though I did do quite a lot of teaching of piano and violin at that time, I still had to have a second job.

WHAT KIND OF MUSIC DID YOU PLAY?

We played dance music. Wasn't all this jumpin' and skylarkin'. . . all the crazy stuff like it is today. It was more orderly dancing, like the waltz, the one-step, the two-step, and the schottische. The music was harmonious during those times. One or two times I played piano with Fletcher Henderson at private events, but I didn't work with him on a regular basis.

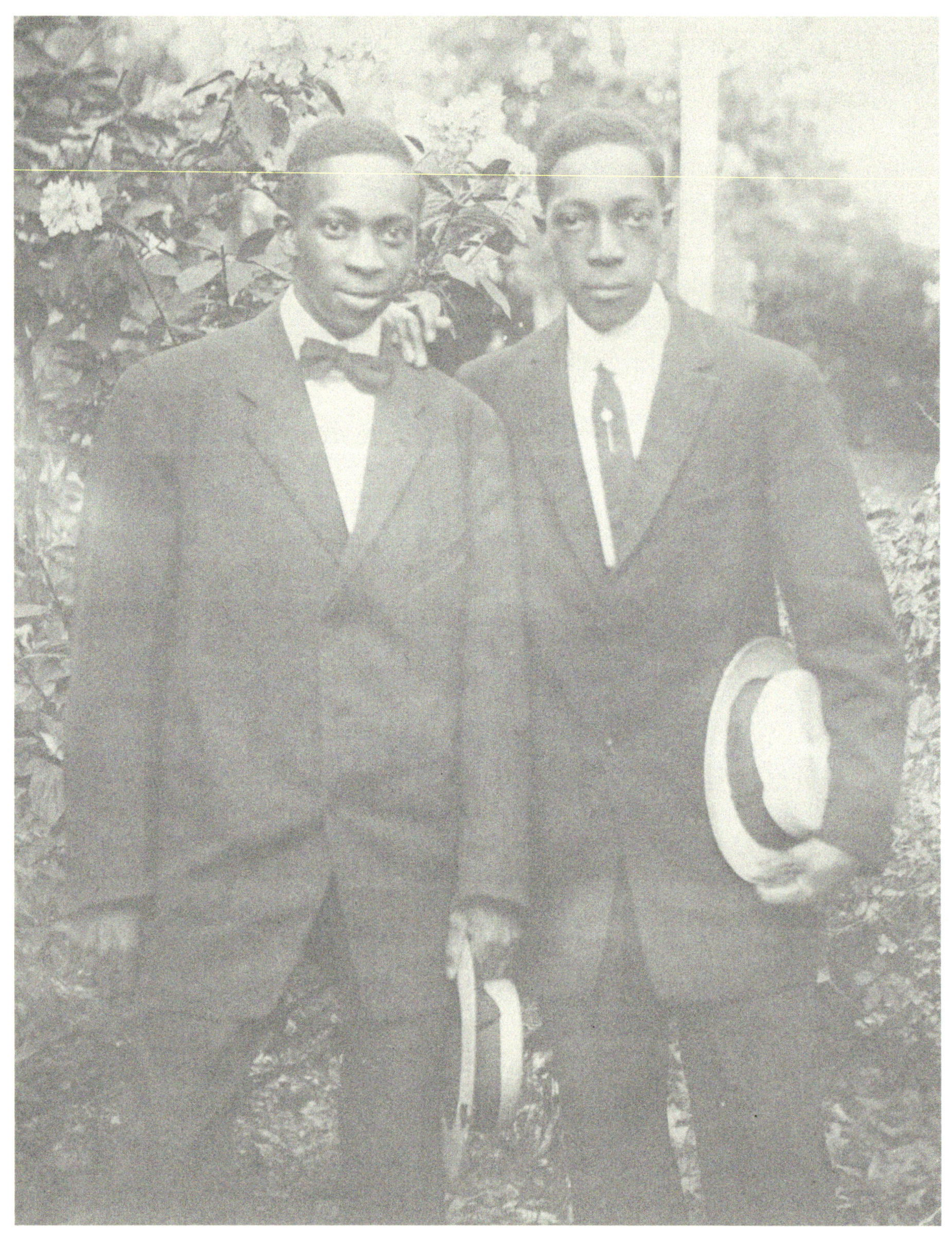

WAS THIS AFTER OR BEFORE YOUR MARRIAGE TO KATE, YOUR FIRST WIFE?

It must have been after. Yeah. I don't know where I was working; it might have been at odd jobs. I think I was working at the Knickerbocker Trust on Thirty-Fourth Street and Fifth Avenue. We were serving meals there for a Mrs. Silverman.

WHO WAS SHE?

Well, she was from Staten Island. She used to furnish meals for the guys that worked at the Knickerbocker Trust. She was very nice. Jack, my father, was working there and so was my brother and I, both. We served one meal a day.

WHAT YEAR WAS THIS? CAN YOU REMEMBER?

Let me see, that was nineteen-seven or -eight.

HOW DID YOU SEE THE WORLD DURING THOSE DAYS?

It just came to me as it was and I accepted it as it was. I made the best of it as I went along, and then finally the picture became prominent and the music business got wavy, and I had to eat regular, so whatever would come along, I did. There'd come a time in the summer when we went home to Lenox, where the hotel there hired a lot of colored waiters and bellboys and so forth. So I went up there summers and made some extra dollars, till one time I got tangled up with a Greek dishwasher. I had a tray that had one big dish on it; one day, the dish flew off and hit the floor, and the echoes through the place sounded like a whole tray full of dishes or somethin', but it was only one dish. The headwaiter came over, and the dishwasher told him that I broke a tray full of dishes. They had made a rule that the waiters would have to pay for their dishes if they broke them. So he told him that I broke a whole tray full of dishes, and I told him that I didn't. I only had had one dish on the tray. He (the dishwasher) was standin' so close to me, he had a prominent nose, that before I knew it, I'd... wasn't nobody goin' to lie about me! The steward of the hotel, why I guess he figured that it was easier to get waiters than it was to get dishwashers; so I was fired. So anyhow, that was the end of that second season of mine at the hotel. So that job taught me patience. Not to be so quick.

Children & the Mystery of Birth

WHAT HAPPENED WHEN YOUR BROTHERS AND SISTERS WERE BORN? WERE YOU AWARE OF YOUR MOTHER'S PREGNANCIES?

You see, I was one of the older ones. Well, my aunt's house was only about fifteen feet away, and when mother was expecting birth—she always had a midwife, who used to come from Pittsfield—my brother and I would stay over to my aunt's house, which was just across the street, in fact.

DID YOU HAVE ANY IDEA OF HOW CHILDREN WERE BORN?

I don't remember when I ever knew or when I ever had any doubts. I know I knew it wasn't no stork bringing them. I don't know how I knew they came. I wasn't like the kid whose mother was expecting who thought she'd tell him that he's gonna have a little playmate pretty soon, so she says to him, "Which would you rather have, William, a baby brother or a little sister?" He said, "Well, I don't know; if you don't think it would put you too much more out of shape, I'd rather have a pony."

DID YOUR FATHER EVER SIT DOWN AND TALK TO YOU ABOUT BIRTH?

No, he didn't.

WHERE DID YOU LEARN ABOUT IT?

From medical books, I guess. I had a natural history well-versed. Let's see, I don't know when a person gets that knowledge and so forth. But I don't feel I ever had any... it's like I don't even know when I first started reading.

WAS YOUR FIRST WIFE'S, KATE'S, PREGNANCY SOMEWHAT OF A MYSTERY TO YOU? WERE YOU CONFUSED?

Well, at first there was a certain amount of bewilderment, but at the same time, it didn't seem to be too much... I don't know, I don't know, I just thought that that's the way it had to be, I guess. Yes, it was kind of surprising to me 'cause I didn't know as much as I know now.

HOW DID YOU FEEL AT THAT TIME?

I don't remember how I felt. Things were happening so fast; we had to go quite a ways to get the doctor. There was no telephones you know, just go runnin' up the street to Dr. Hale. He's the one who attended her. He was the town's doctor in Lenox, Massachusetts. The child was born in September.

DID YOU SEE YOUR CHILD BORN?

No. The doctor came, and he said that it'd be some time. So he went out back. In the meantime, the pains had been increasing and so forth; so I went out to get him. When we came back, why she had already given birth.

TO RACHEL?

Yes. But as I said, she seemed to have had some experience. She had already given birth when the doctor got back, and all she had to do was to... well, I wasn't up in the room. I don't know.

WHEN DID THE SECOND CHILD, EMILE, COME?

I think he came when we was living in the Victoria Apartments on Lenox Avenue [in New York City] at that time. He only lived a year, and I didn't get a chance to know too much about him.

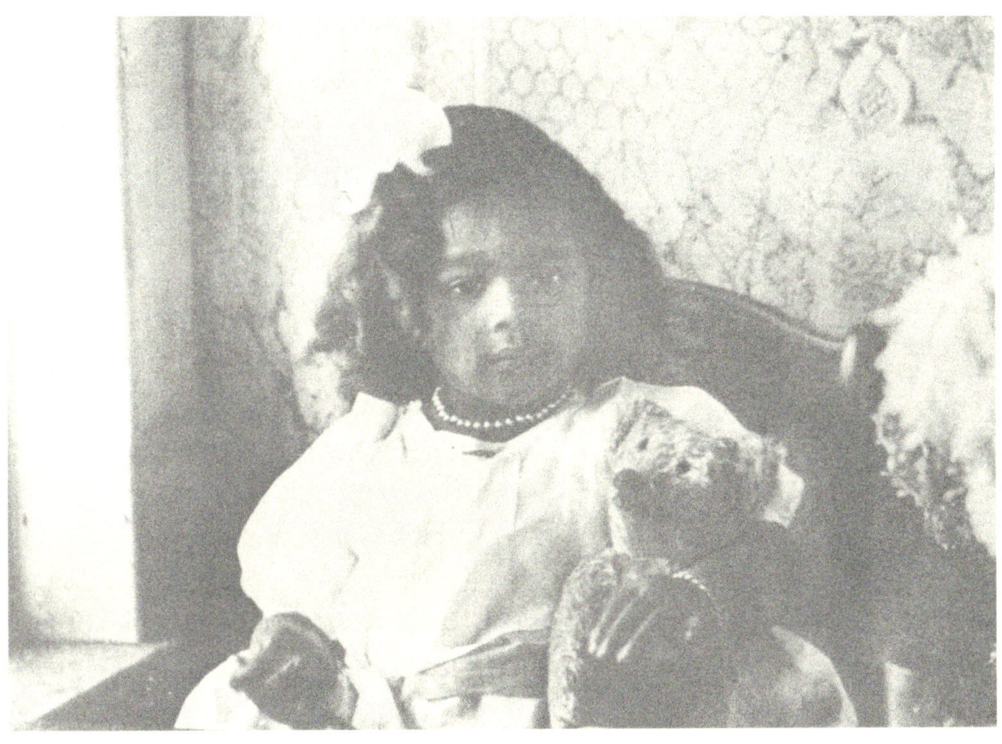

Yes, I have a couple of pictures of him.

WHEN KATE WAS PREGNANT WITH EMILE, WHAT DID YOU THINK ABOUT HAVING CHILDREN?

Well, I felt as they came, I tried to make the best of it. I had previously intended to go to school to study languages and continue my music and so forth; so when I saw it was the other way, I could see all my plans and bubbles going up in the air and bursting.

DID PEOPLE PLAN FOR CHILDREN DURING THOSE TIMES, OR DID THEY JUST COME?

They didn't plan too much. I didn't do no planning, I just knew he was coming and made arrangements for it and accepted it, I guess.

DID YOU THINK THAT CHILDREN WERE A BURDEN?

They did require attention but I don't think they grew up as fast as they do today. During that time Kate had no steady job, so most of it was dependent on me, because the money wasn't so plentiful in those days and you couldn't do both, raise a family and have a career, too; I'd have to sacrifice something. When Rachel was young I'd taken a lot of pictures of her and Kate.

HOW OLD WAS RACHEL WHEN YOU AND KATE WERE DIVORCED?

I think she was about eight years old. After that she lived with her mother.

BOTH OF YOUR CHILDREN DIED YOUNG, DIDN'T THEY, MR. VAN DER ZEE?

Yes, my second child, Emile, he died when he was a little over a year old, and Rachel, she died around the time she was 16 years old.

YOU PHOTOGRAPHED RACHEL'S FUNERAL, DIDN'T YOU?

Yes.

DIDN'T YOU FIND IT HARD TO PHOTOGRAPH RACHEL IN THE COFFIN?

Not as I recall because she hadn't been with me at the time. Her mother had taken her up to Maine during the summers. She had just graduated from school when she was stricken with appendicitis. I have some very nice watercolor pictures that Rachel painted before she died.

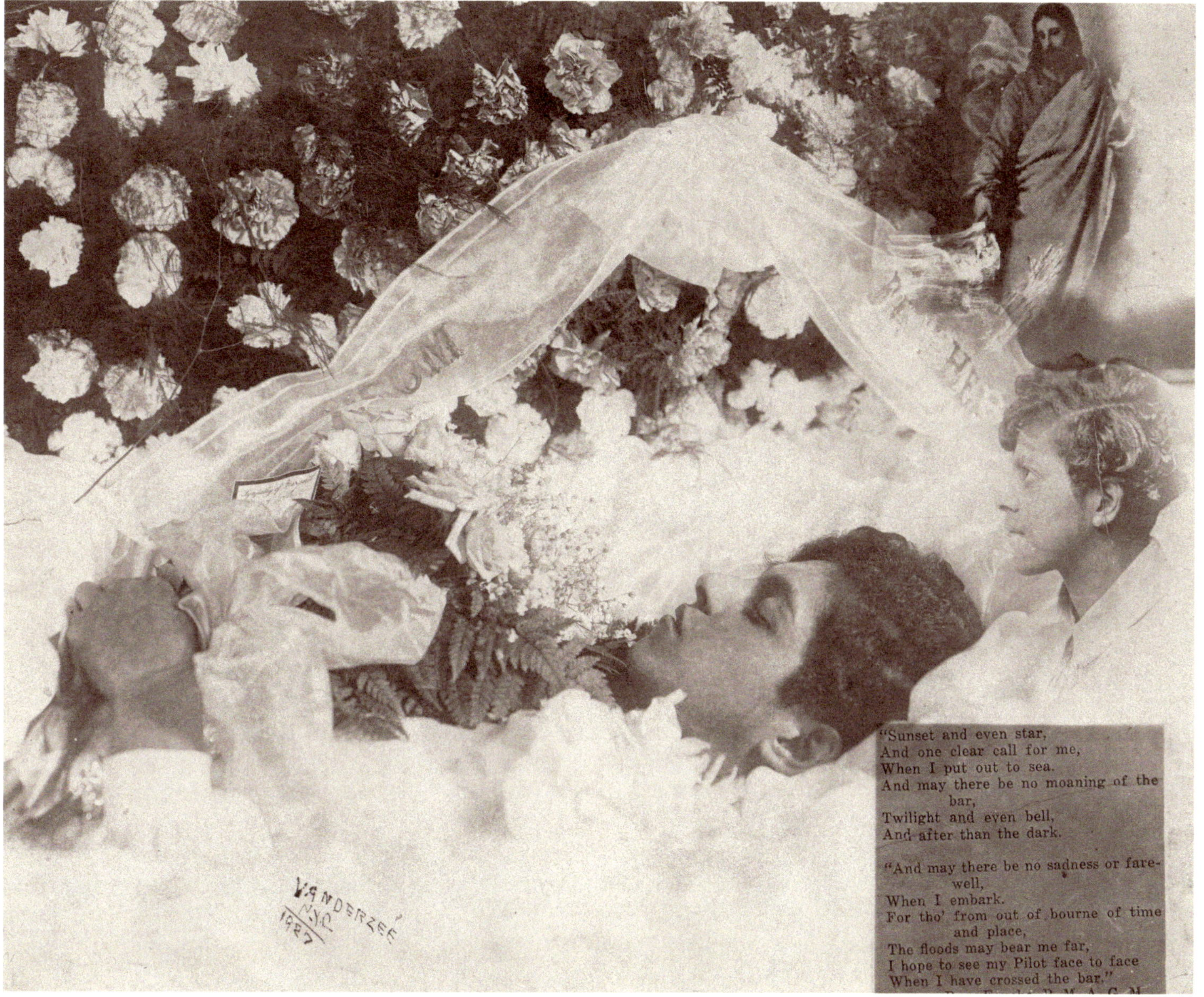

Rachel Van Der Zee

WHAT WERE YOUR FEELINGS ABOUT HER FUNERAL?

I really don't remember. It was a beautiful funeral 'cause all the young girls there were all about her age. She belonged to some club that they all belonged to. It was a very nice funeral. I don't know, I think Rachel's funeral was done at Madame Lane's Funeral Parlor on 136th Street, between Lenox and Seventh Avenue on the downtown side of the street. I don't know whether it's still there or not; it's four or five funeral parlors there.

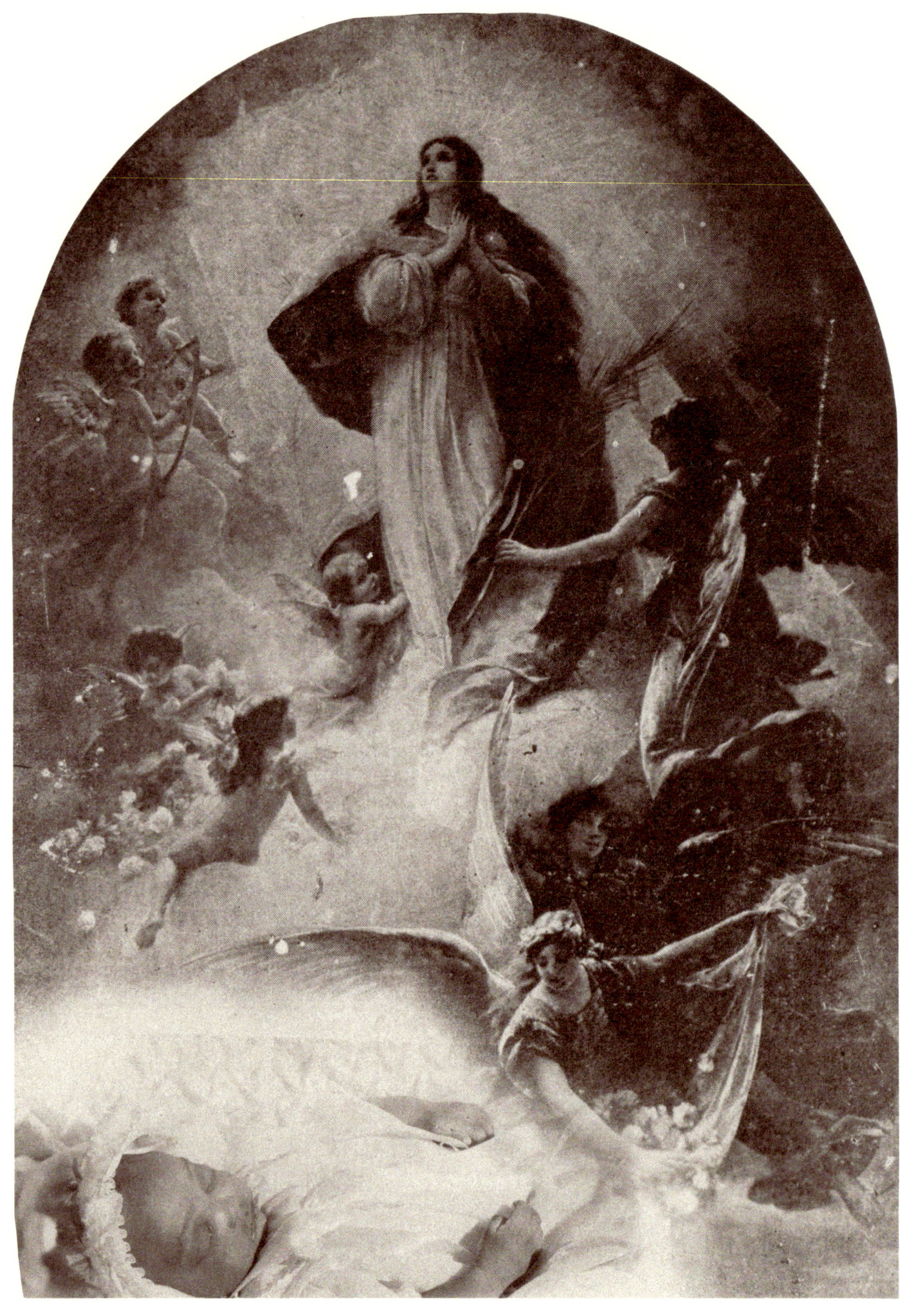

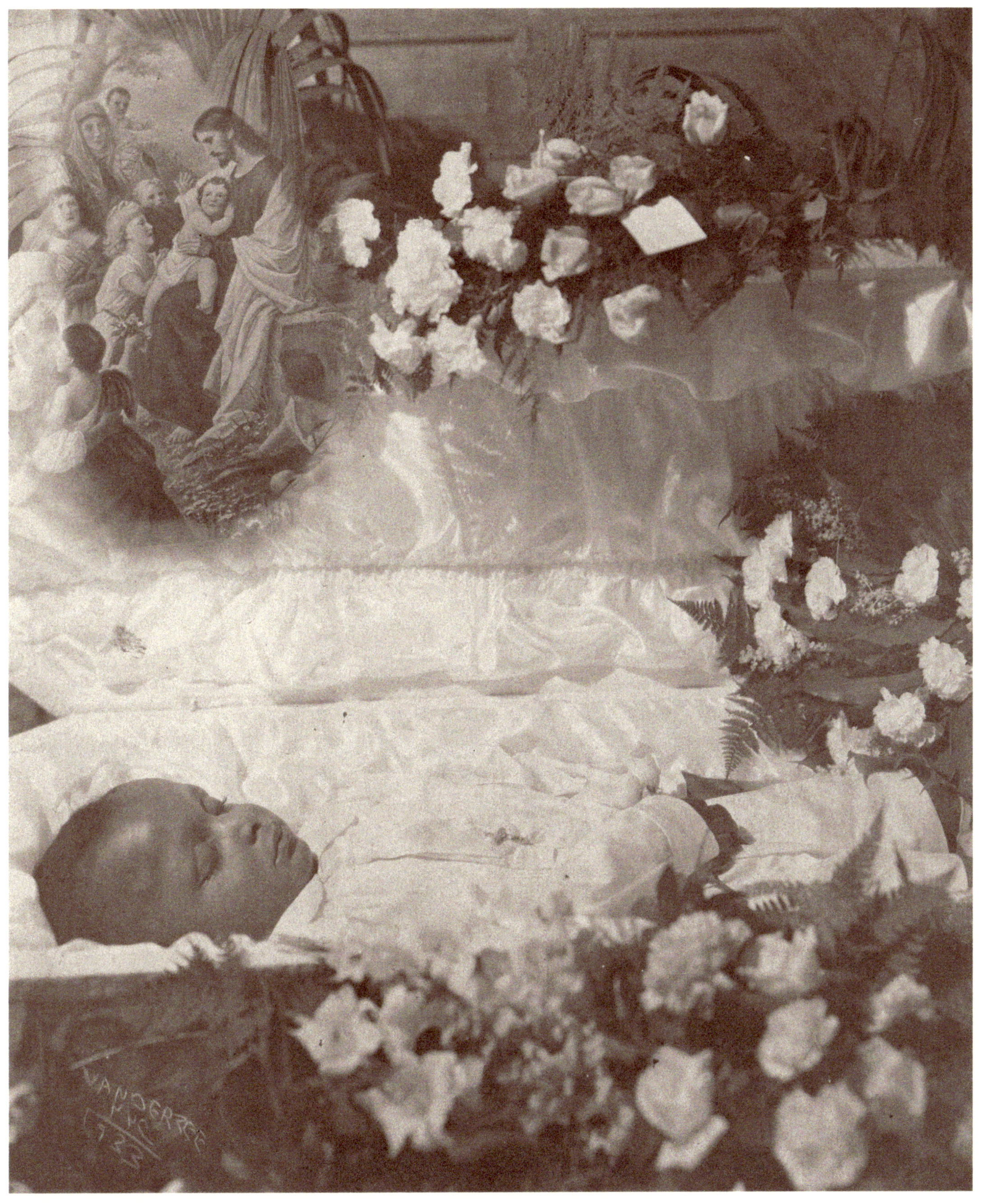
VANDERZEE

You'll always be my baby now,
Johnella. Dream sometimes of Papa.
When you marry an angel boy,
The very best,
I'll attend your wedding.

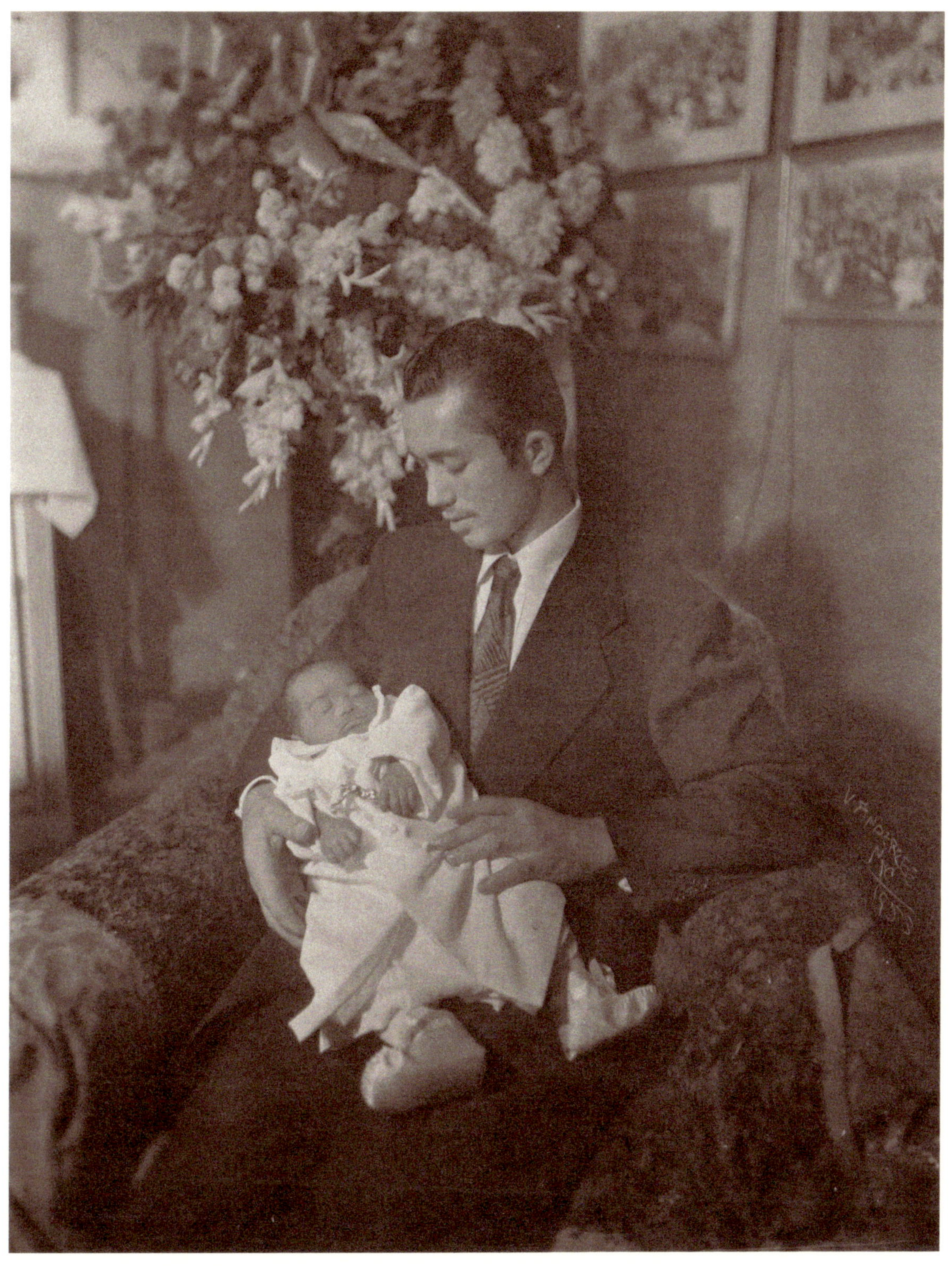

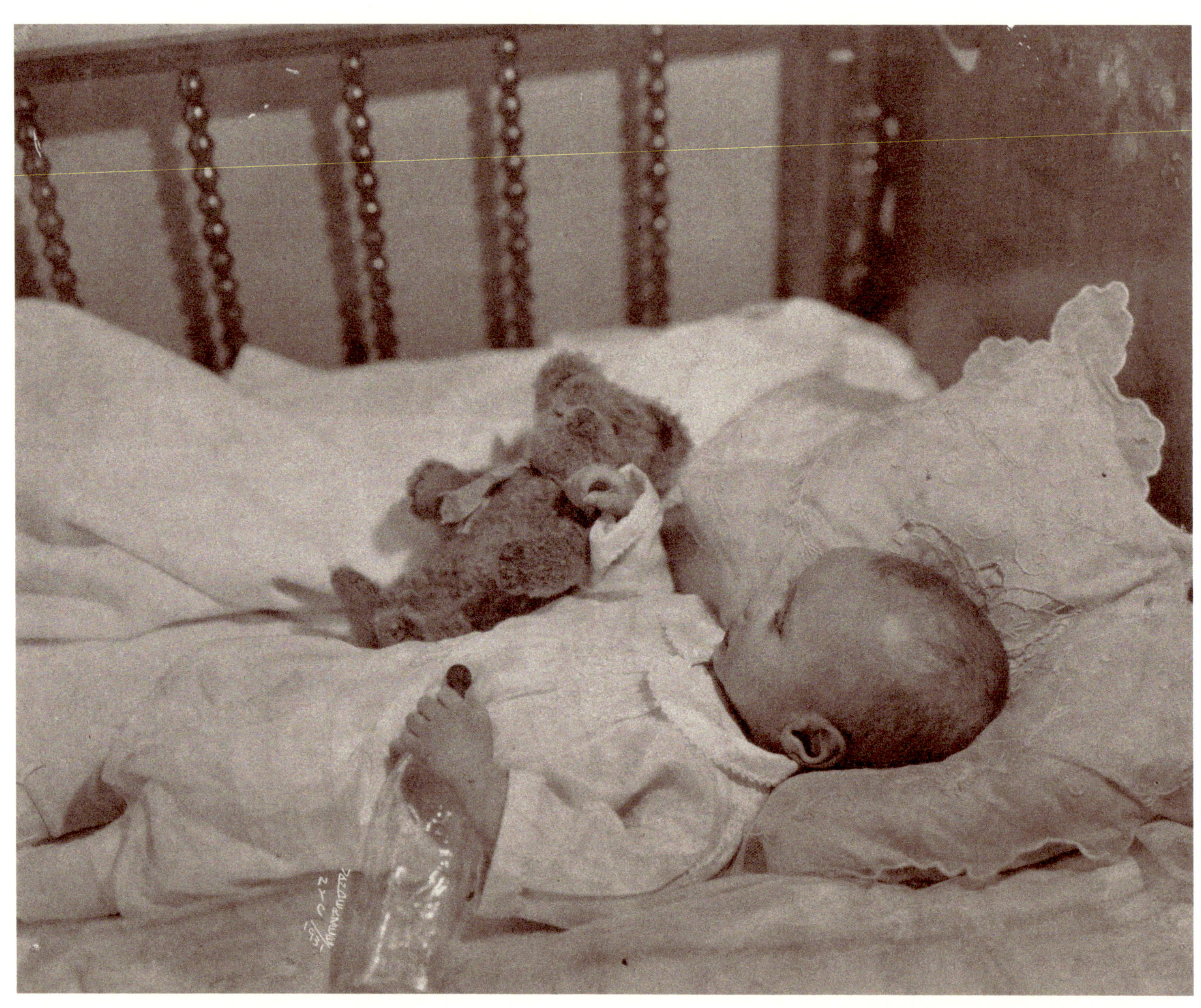

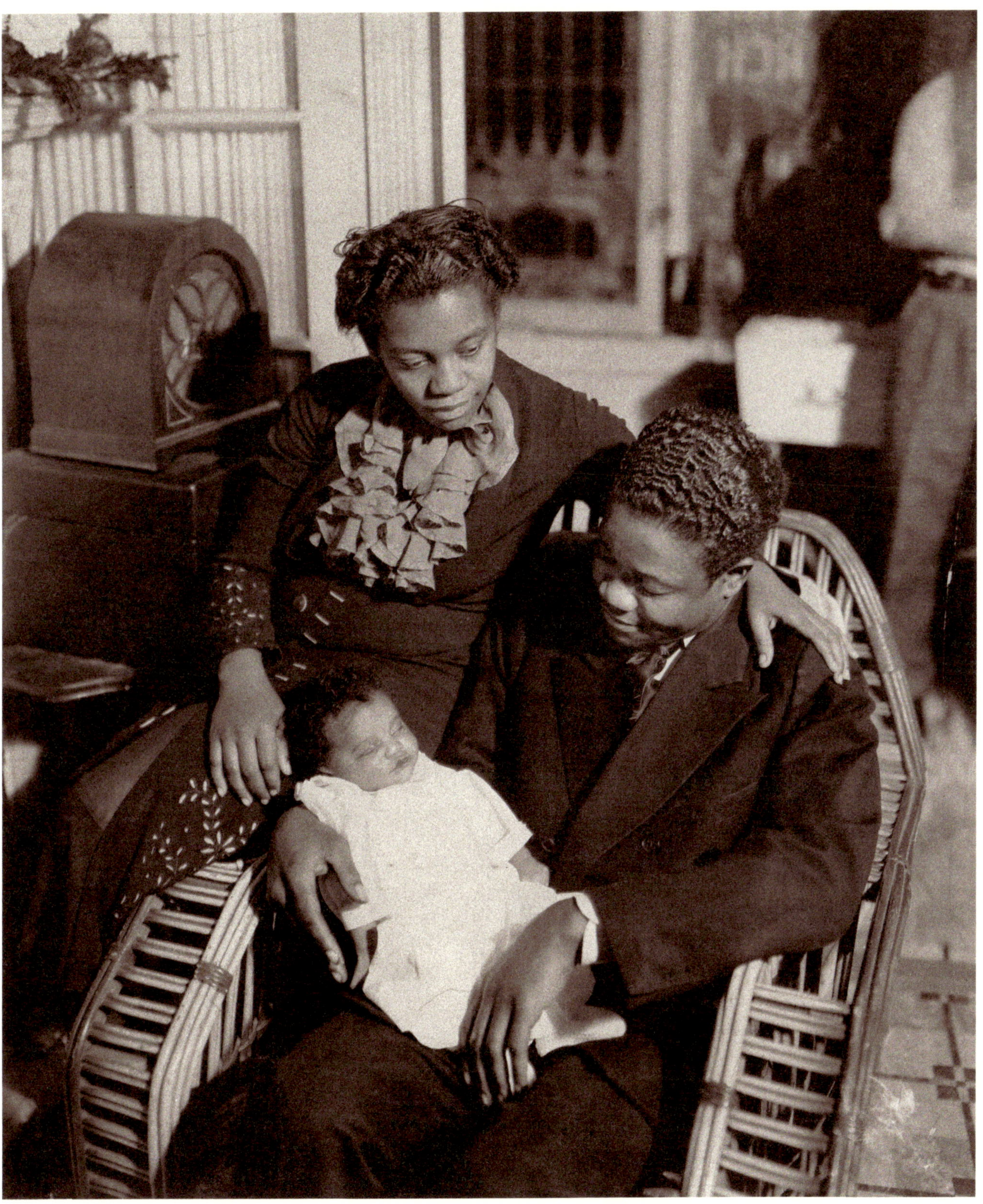

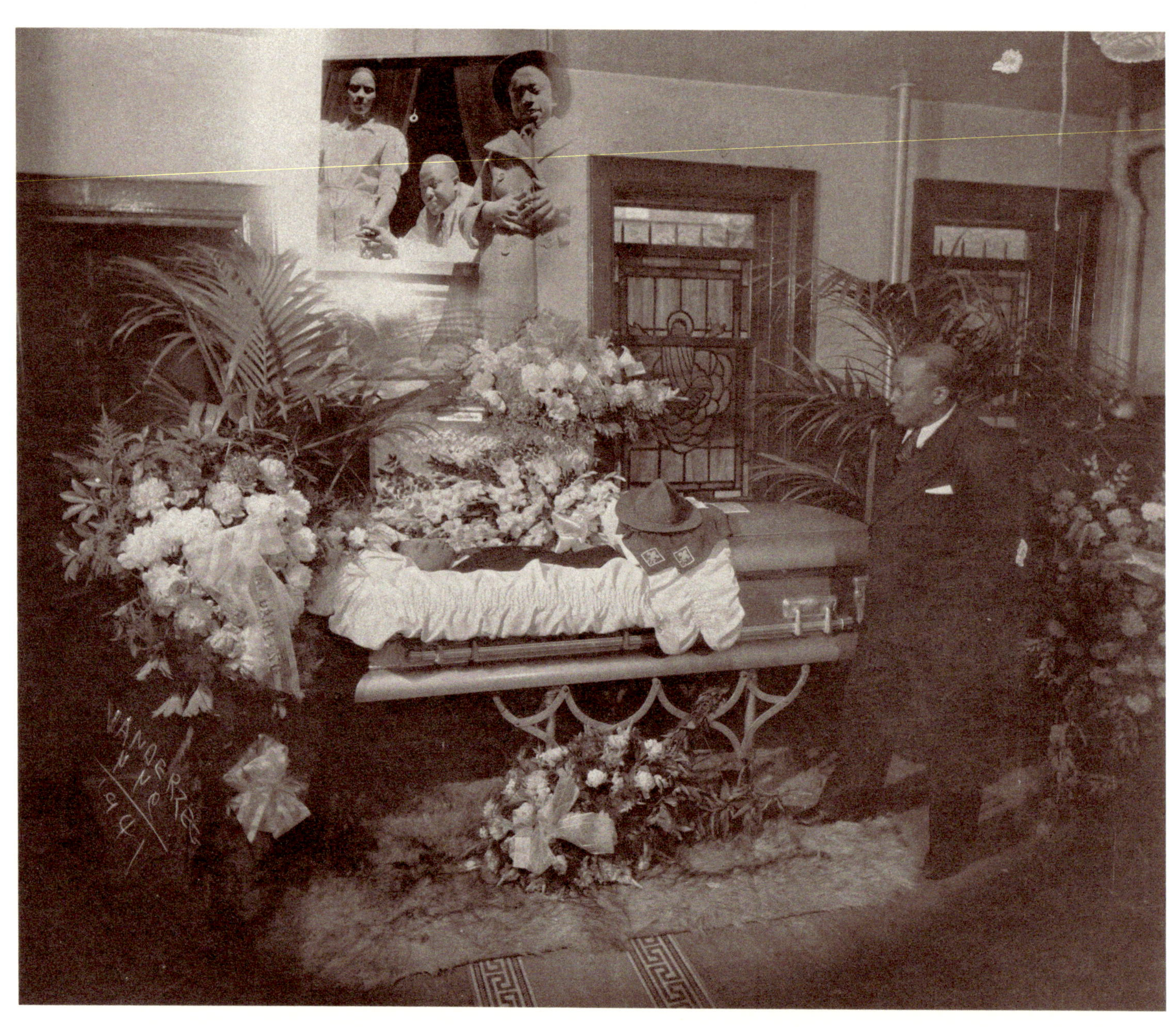

Can I use my boy scout knife
To carve the bark of birch trees
And send cards to Mama and Popa
Signed with your name and mine,
Jesus, do you think?

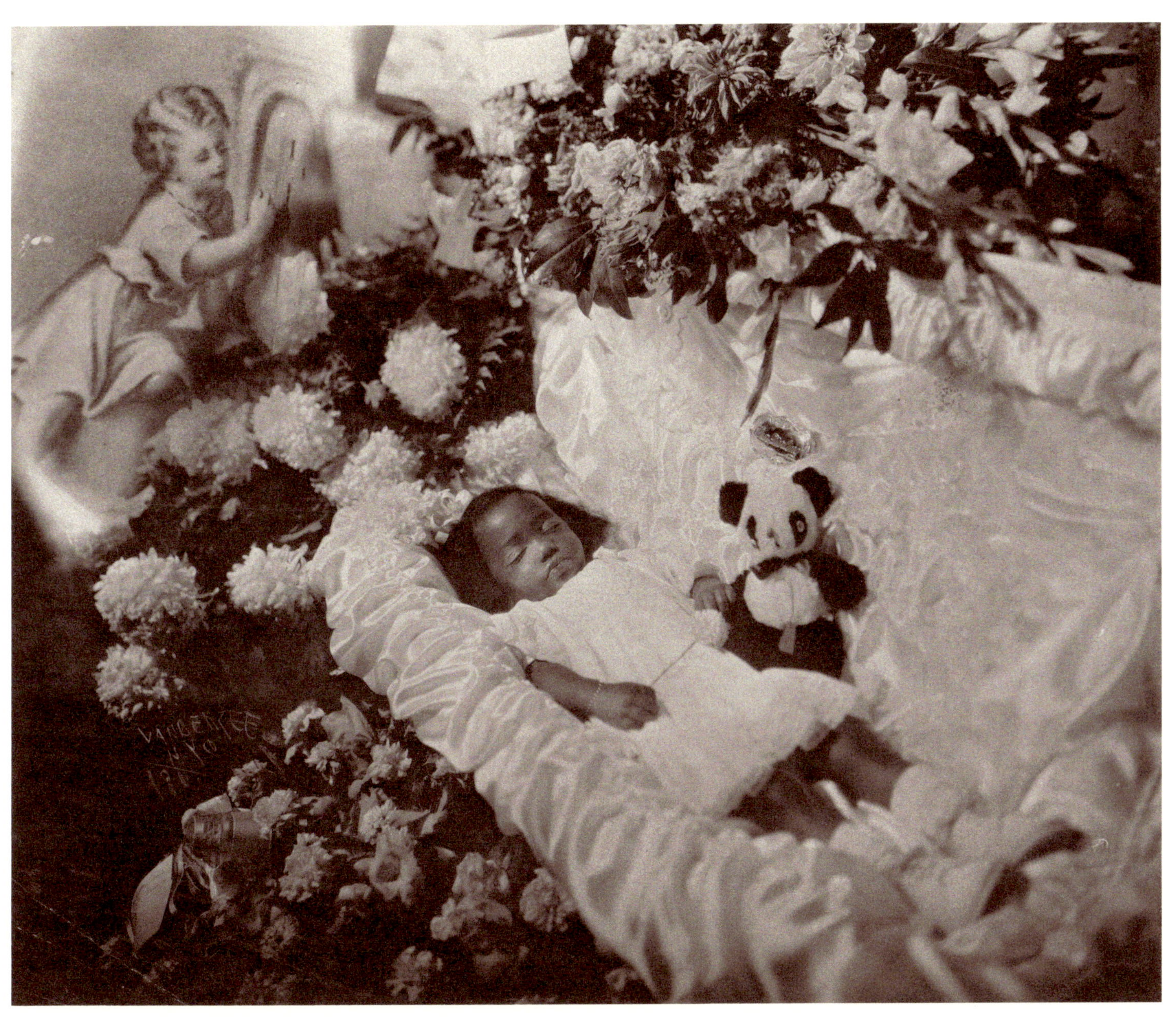

At least
I got me a new dress
An' a hair ribbon
Like a bluebird.

The Children

There's poison in the Christmas
peppermint
Kids will never dance again.
Their dying is our sin.
We'll never sleep again.
Their jump ropes turned to
snakes.
They'll never skip again.
The strangling is our sin.
We'll never sleep again.
Little children, little children,
Trust us just once more.
Little children, little children,
Stop knocking at our door.
We'll never sleep again.
We are the rich, we are the
poor
We'll never sleep again.
Stop pounding on our door!

Women: Wives & Friends

DID KATE REMIND YOU OF ANY OF THE WOMEN IN YOUR FAMILY, OR WAS SHE DIFFERENT?

Very much the same, I guess. She had a mind of her own; she was good at making the decisions and so forth. I had no experience along those lines.

YOUR MARRIAGE TO KATE HAD A STORMY BEGINNING, DIDN'T IT?

Well, she was pregnant, I mean that's why I married her.

DID YOU FEEL THAT YOU WERE FORCED INTO MARRIAGE?

No, I wasn't forced into it. Since it was my child, why, then, I'd be man enough to stand by it. When she said, "No, I don't believe people get along well with marrying under those circumstances," she said that she'd go on about her business, and forget about it. Well, so you say, "It's mine, and so I do that." Well, so, finally I talked her into it. She got ahold of a Reverend Doctor Simms or somebody, and he performed the necessary requirements to make us one. Then I felt at the time that I'd never thought about getting a room rental. I got a thought from an ad, get an apartment. So that was kind of how it was. But I guess, at that time, I wasn't used to taking care of anybody. I had just come out of a home and was used to people looking out for me, and taking care of me, and so I figured it was a new experience for me. I hunted around and I finally found an apartment on Twenty-Ninth Street in New York, which was a pretty nice street then. The rent was twenty-nine dollars, which was an awful lot of money at that time, because I wasn't used to paying these monthly rents and stuff. Why, at my parents' home we had our own home and without any rent, although I did hear once about paying some taxes or something like that.

WHAT KIND OF APARTMENT DID YOU GET?

I ended up with what you'd call a "railroad flat" with two doors, and that meant you had to have two locks. I think I had about three bank accounts and about twenty dollars in all three of them. So, anyhow, I managed. It was a cold water flat, and that meant you had to heat your own water by boiling it over the top of the stove. The old coal-and-wood man used to come around and sell stuff for the fire. So I bought the locks and put the locks on the door and put wood in the stove. There was nothing in the place; so I told Kate to go and get a table. We got a table, but it didn't have no chairs, and then we got the chairs and then we didn't have no springs or mattress; so we got that...so I said, "What on earth is this?" So I saw my few dollars dwindling away.

WHEN YOU AND KATE GOT MARRIED, DID YOU HAVE A WEDDING LIKE THE BRIDES IN YOUR PHOTOGRAPHS?

No, no, we didn't have any of that kind of business.

WHY NOT?

Didn't see the necessity of it.

WERE YOU PHOTOGRAPHING THEN?

Well, not to any great extent. I did, you know, just a little private work with a 4x5 camera at that time, although I didn't charge for it. I'd talk with Kate about going into business, but she said, "No. You'd better get a job, then you'll know where your money's coming from." She wasn't as progressive as the second wife. At that time, you could only get eight to ten dollars a week. Kate was a seamstress and gown maker at some seminary on Twenty-Third Street, I believe. I had no experience, but she seemed to have had quite a lot of experience.

DO YOU REMEMBER SOME OF THE "BRIDE" PICTURES THAT YOU TOOK?

The "bride" styles changed, and so did the way in which I took the pictures. One time, they wore short dresses; another time, they had long trains. There was one couple that never did get their pictures. They broke up before they got the pictures. I remember the girl said she got married down at City Hall. She had come all the way up on the subway with her gown and train. She had sneakers on under her gown. It would have been kind of embarrassing to me to be on the train. Then a few weeks later, she come back to see if he'd been after the pictures or not. She said that he had taken her trunk and moved. I didn't try to get in touch with them, didn't see any sense but I did meet her a few times after that, about three or four years later. I don't know where she is now.

YOU SPENT A LOT OF TIME ON YOUR PHOTOGRAPHS. WHAT WAS ONE OF YOUR CONCEPTS OF BEAUTY IN PEOPLE?

Well, I could always see beauty where it didn't exist. And I figured, as long as they had two eyes and a nose and a mouth, why I could improve on them. On some of them, you'd cut down the mouth or sharpen up the nose.

DID SOME OF THEM ACTUALLY COME UP AND SAY, "I WANT YOU TO FIX MY MOUTH AND MAKE ME PRETTIER" OR DID YOU DO IT AUTOMATICALLY?

Well, they'd want to know why the pictures were better lookin' than they were. Then I'd go in and show them the lines and the crow's-feet, double chins, and all of that stuff. Some of them who would have pictures made without retouching done on them would say later, "That man don't know how to make pictures." And next time, they'd be back to me to have me do them again. Where they had certain characteristic lines, why, I'd tone them down, soften them up so they wouldn't be so conspicuous. If they had gaps in their front teeth, why, I'd close them up a little bit. Some of them were cross-eyed, I'd straighten out the eyes. I always put the people in a position that showed them to the most advantage.

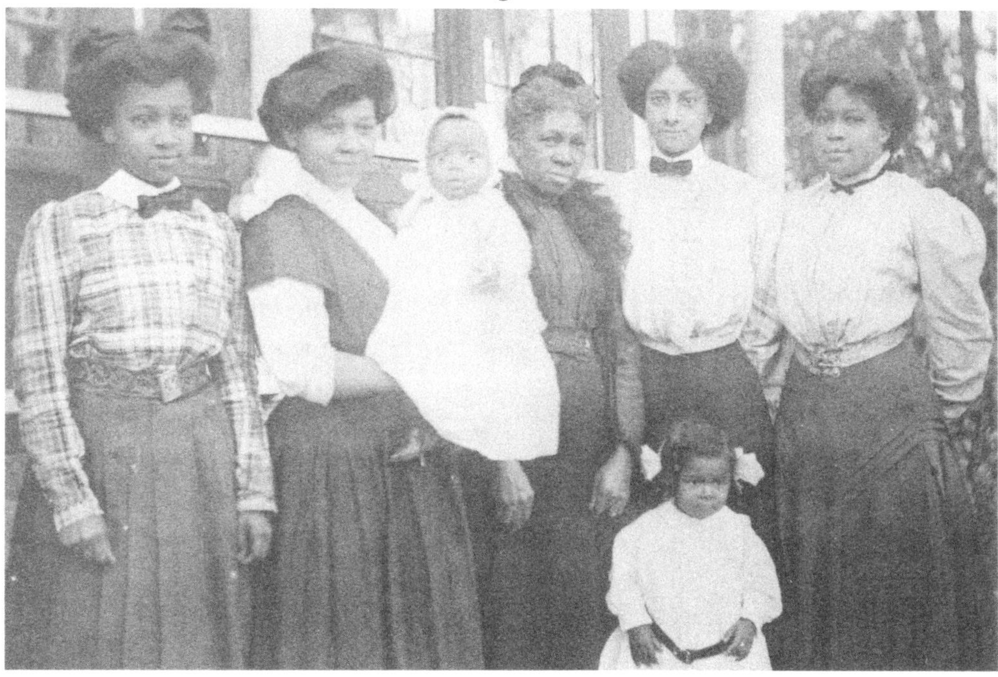

I'D LIKE TO RETURN TO YOUR RELATIONSHIP WITH KATE. WHERE DID YOU MEET HER?

I was playing a solo at one of the churches. After the service there, she was standing back at the back of the hall of the church, waiting to congratulate me and tell me how much she enjoyed it. I think then I got her address and formed an acquaintance which I think was a very short duration before I thought I'd play the man and take her out and that's what happened. Next time I saw her, she said, "I believe you ruined me."

OH, MY GOODNESS!

Well, that was a shock to me; so it was up to me to be responsible.

DID YOU MARRY KATE BECAUSE YOUR PARENTS HAD TAUGHT YOU RESPONSIBILITY?

Well, you could say so. She wasn't bad. She looked all right to me, but I wasn't figuring on gettin' married right away. I thought I had had no intentions to get married until I had at least $500 in the bank, which at that time was quite a substantial amount. But since I figured out it was my fault, that was it. We got married in New York.

WERE YOU AND KATE ABOUT THE SAME AGE WHEN YOU MARRIED?

I must have been older, but she had had more experience because she was working out when I met her.

WHAT DO YOU MEAN?

She'd been out working, I don't know how many years 'round places, whereas I had just come from home.

ABOUT HOW OLD WERE YOU?

About twenty, I guess.

DID YOUR WIFE CONTINUE TO WORK AFTER YOU GOT MARRIED?

She did quite a lot of sewing around different people. Yeah, she'd be sewing and making all of Rachel's clothes and things and a great many of her own.

DID YOU LIKE BEING MARRIED, MR. VAN DER ZEE?

No, I can't say I didn't like it. I just knew I had married and that was it; I had to accept it.

YOU DON'T SOUND AS IF YOU WERE TOO HAPPY ABOUT IT.

Well, it kind of came on ahead of time. I don't think that I had enough outside experience before I was married.

WHY DID YOU AND KATE BREAK UP?

One of the reasons, besides her wanting to leave every summer, was that she had another guy used to come up there, a friend of mine. I guess they probably had...'cause I know when I was going to work sometime, he'd been there half of the day. His name was Harry Montgomery. I was supposed to go to work at a certain time, but I didn't get out as soon as I expected; he'd been there all the afternoon, and finally there come a knock on the door and here he was back again. So I was surprised to see him back; I didn't know what was comin' off. "Well, um, I'm surprised," he said. "Well," I said, "you was here all the afternoon, and you're comin' back here now." I began to understand that when I was working nights, sometimes she'd just be over at her boyfriend's across the street or some other place.

WHAT HAPPENED AFTER SHE MOVED OUT?

Well, I know that I was living more of a lively life than it had been with her. At that time I had a boy who was livin' with me who was a piano player. We'd put out little parties and so forth, and finally I began to worry that she [Kate] might come back. She did come back, but she stayed with a girl friend of hers, a Miss Diane Royal, who was in the real estate business. We never did get together after that.

We were mis-mated, I guess. Now, I liked Kate. I never would have quit her...I don't say that I probably wouldn't have done some two-timin' because every time I'd pick a sweetie, a sweeter sweetie'd come along and change my mind. But every song, it can have two or three endings.

WERE YOU A LADIES' MAN?

Well, there was one or two that I liked very much, that I never could seem to get started with.

WAS THIS WHILE YOU WERE MARRIED TO KATE?

This was before I married Kate. Her name was Mrs. Rosalie and she lived on Fifty-Second Street. Rosalie somethin', I can't think of her last name now. Anyhow, I bought tickets to the show and I thought I'd go by and take her to the show; so I went by and I knocked on the door, and her mother came to the door, and I asked, "Is Rosalie in?" "Rosalie? Haven't you heard about Rosalie?" "No, I haven't heard nothing about Rosalie." "Why, Rosalie, she was married to George Hornby last Thursday." Well. That was news to me, 'cause I hadn't seen anyone else around. I thought I was the only pebble on her beach at the time, I guess. So then I scuttled down the street to another woman I knew down there, Frankie Marshall. So she was home at the time, so we went to the show. Then there was another girl named Mimi Hatfield. I liked her very much, but I couldn't seem to contact her. I had just come from Lenox, and there was so many nice women around there in New York that I was lookin' over the situation. Then I got tangled up in my own mess, I guess.

HOW DID YOU MEET GAYNELLA, YOUR SECOND WIFE?

I was working at an apartment house at Forty-Four West Seventy-Second Street, where Gaynella was a telephone operator.

IS THAT THE SAME TIME THAT YOU MET ROXY?

Yeah. Roxy was a maid of one of the tenants there and Gaynella was a relief operator. The maids would give me more meals than I wanted, so I'd carry food down to Gaynella. At that time she had an apartment on Thirty-Fourth Street, which she paid about fourteen, seventeen dollars a month for.

WHAT ABOUT YOUR RELATIONSHIPS WITH ROXY & GAYNELLA?

I was seein' both of them, runnin' one days and the other one nights. Finally they caught up with me one time. They said that it was time I made up my mind which one I wanted. Well, I liked them both, and I couldn't very well travel between them; so the quickest way I could get out of it was by saying, "I don't like either damn one," and I left them to stew in their dilemma.

DID YOU FEEL THAT WOMEN PRACTICED SOME KIND OF MAGIC ON MEN OR HAD CONTROL OF THEM OR SOMETHING?

Some women, as I said, have more influence than others.

WHAT DO YOU MEAN?

They're more persistent, persuasive, in a way of speaking. Give you more confidence. I see women as an inspiration, something to work for. It don't take a whole lot to satisfy a man. A woman gives a man something to go on, otherwise he's like a ship without a rudder with nobody to lead him on and give him inspiration.

DO YOU THINK THAT WOMEN DRIVE MEN TOO FAR, SOMETIMES?

Some of them do, and that's why some men may have heart attacks, as it may be. But they don't want to lose the woman, and they find out that somebody else's got more than he's got, then he's got to get more to satisfy her wants and needs, and in some cases it's just that the woman and man weren't properly mated, I guess.

TOWARD THE END OF YOUR MARRIAGE, YOU TOLD ME, KATE TRIED TO GET YOU DRAFTED.

She didn't care whether it was 369th or 370th or whatever [regiment] it was, as long as I was in the Army. They were drafting people during that time but I managed to duck it myself. Though the wife was trying her best to get me in there. She wrote them [the World War I draft board] that I was a strong, able-bodied man and she didn't see why they didn't take me. Well, I had a mother living, so I got an exemption on account of her. Besides, my wife couldn't prove my exact age.

DID YOU EVER ASK KATE WHY SHE DID THAT?

I didn't ask her why she did it, but I knew it was because of the time I had thrown a scare into her about breaking up of the household every summer that she went down to Virginia. I had told her "The next time you go, don't come back." Sure enough, a few days after that, I come home and she had packed up everything and gone. She left me a note saying that I said that if she would be going home to Virginia all the time, why, next thing we'd be quarreling and fighting and there was no sense to that; so she thought that before that time'd come she'd leave. But she'd said in the beginning, "I don't think that people that ever got married the way we did got along very well together." So she must have intended to leave anyhow. Well, I felt kind of sad for awhile but everyone would come up there and visit me so it wasn't so bad.

WHAT HAPPENED NEXT?

Then Kate and I went to court. She had me payin' alimony when I tried to open up the studio. She said that I was makin' plenty of money, and I was, so she wanted alimony. The lawyer who was supposed to be my lawyer, came one day when I was openin' up the studio and served me with a summons. He was the lawyer that I had hired and now he was workin' for Kate. He had told her, "Your husband's thinkin' about gettin' a divorce; the best thing you can do is serve papers on him quick." So they had me payin' two hundred and fifty dollars counsel fees and forty dollars a week alimony. That was a lot of money at that time. Of course, I had the studio by then, but even so, it was a lot of money. And every once in a while, I took a walk downtown to look at the Ludlow Jail, where the alimony guys who didn't keep up to date was confined. Before the case was settled, why, the judge died, and the next one didn't know how to assign the responsibility; so they had to have a retrial. So the next judge come along, and he threw it out. So then, that relieved me of that. I was lucky. I didn't have to pay alimony or support or nothing. In the meantime, Kate went down south and got some kind of divorce down there. She married another fellow by the name of White.

YOUR MARRIAGE TO GAYNELLA WAS EASIER THAN THE ONE YOU HAD SHARED WITH KATE, WASN'T IT?

By that time I had had more experience at the thing. Gaynella was married at the time I met her and so was I. She was married to a fellow by the name of Charles Greenlee, who was a kind of a frail, sickly fellow. He worked for Regal Shoe Store there down on Thirty-Fifth Street. He also had people up in Mount Vernon or somewheres up there and quite a large family over in Greenlakes, too.

BEFORE YOU MARRIED GAYNELLA, YOU WERE SEEING ROXY, TOO. HOW DID YOU SEE THE TWO WOMEN?

Roxy was very sincere, she liked me very much. It seemed like she wasn't as good a housekeeper as Gaynella was. Gaynella was much better lookin' than Roxy was. And I couldn't understand such a pretty girl (Roxy was a maid) gettin' down on her knees and scrubbin' floors up. Both Roxy and Gaynella had nice homes, but Roxy never did much cooking for me. Now Gaynella, she had me over there and had a nice steak and mashed potatoes all swimming in butter and everything. Another time she cooked some corned beef that was pretty good.

WELL, DID SHE GET TO YOU THROUGH YOUR STOMACH?

She had me comin' and goin' over there to her house, and as I said before, most of the time her husband was sickly and up to his people's home up in Mount Vernon there. So I was quick to go by there. She'd have these nice meals for me—and I liked to eat in those days. The food used to taste so good. She was the first person I've seen to cook five or six eggs at a time. I was talking to her and meeting her daily. She had me up there to dinner at different times, but I... I don't know, it all happened in the background. That's all past so long and so far. So far back. Sixty-five years ago. Wooh!

YES, BUT YOU STILL REMEMBER HOW MANY EGGS SHE COOKED!

Well, she was the first one I ever seen cook so many eggs like that. I was just used to two eggs, and I said, "Look! She's got me eatin' five or six eggs at a time."

YOU'VE FORGOTTEN EVERYTHING ELSE BUT THE EGGS.

That was one of the most impressive things that she ever did. She liked to eat. She ate the best of steaks and stuff. We were all kind of short of money around those times. I never had much money, but she was liberal with her money. Then finally, after Kate had left, Gaynella decided it would be good for me to come and live with her and her husband. When we moved out of there, we got a bigger apartment. Her husband, who had been sickly, didn't live too much longer after that. Gaynella was a good provider and had such good ideas; she saw higher than I did. One of the studios she picked out, I couldn't understand. I told her, "What do you want that big old garage for?" She saw possibilities in it that I couldn't see or hadn't thought about. It turned out to be a wonderful studio. It was called the Guaranteed Photo Studio. Then, when we incorporated, the lawyer said that nobody could use that name except banks and trust companies. I don't know why, but anyway I told Gaynella that we'd name the studio after her name [GGG] for Gaynella Grenley Greenlee. I felt a certain amount of confidence with her by my side.

WERE YOU MARRIED TO GAYNELLA DURING THAT TIME?

No, I wasn't married then. First off, Kate was still living when I opened up the studio so we made it appear as if I was an employee and Gaynella was the manager. Because Kate might make trouble and sue

Gaynella for alienation of affection or something.

YOUR LIFE WITH GAYNELLA WAS A LONG ONE WASN'T IT?

Yes, we had a full life. A nice home up on 272 Lenox Avenue between 124th and 123rd Street with fourteen rooms, radios. We took roomers from time to time. But all life is not a good life and, as the poet says, "Into each life some rain must fall"—some fell in ours. We had some bad times with a lawyer who was supposed to be representing us and, as they say, to make a long story short, we lost the house of forty-three years to the bank. It caused the Missus to lose her mind. The marshall put all of our earthly belongings on the sidewalk. I even took a picture of it. But as they say, things which seem to be a curse, sometimes are blessings in disguise.

WHAT DO YOU MEAN?

Well right along through there Reginald McGhee'd taken my photographs to be included with the "Harlem On My Mind" exhibition [at the Metropolitan Museum of Art in 1968-9]. Lot of people became interested in my pictures after that.

WHAT HAPPENED AFTER YOU LOST YOUR HOUSE?

We had to take temporary quarters in a welfare hotel on Concord Place and 260th Street in the Bronx. But after awhile we couldn't stay there because we hadn't been burned out of our house, so we didn't qualify for welfare service, and I had to pay rent there at a hundred and forty dollars per week. There was maid service and bellboys, but no cooking. The relocation people got us where I am today here on West Ninety-Fourth Street.

DID GAYNELLA EVER REGAIN HER SANITY?

Well, the problem she had was her memory. She couldn't remember anything. In her last years she was difficult; but then, for so many years she had been a good wife. She died in June, 1976. She was no trouble to live with, but she also wasn't herself.

DID YOU GO TO YOUR WIFE'S FUNERAL?

No, it was very sad. A photographer named Frank Stewart took a picture of her for me. It's a nice photograph, but I'm going to make some improvements on it when I get straightened out. Now I just keep flowers around her picture and try to forget.

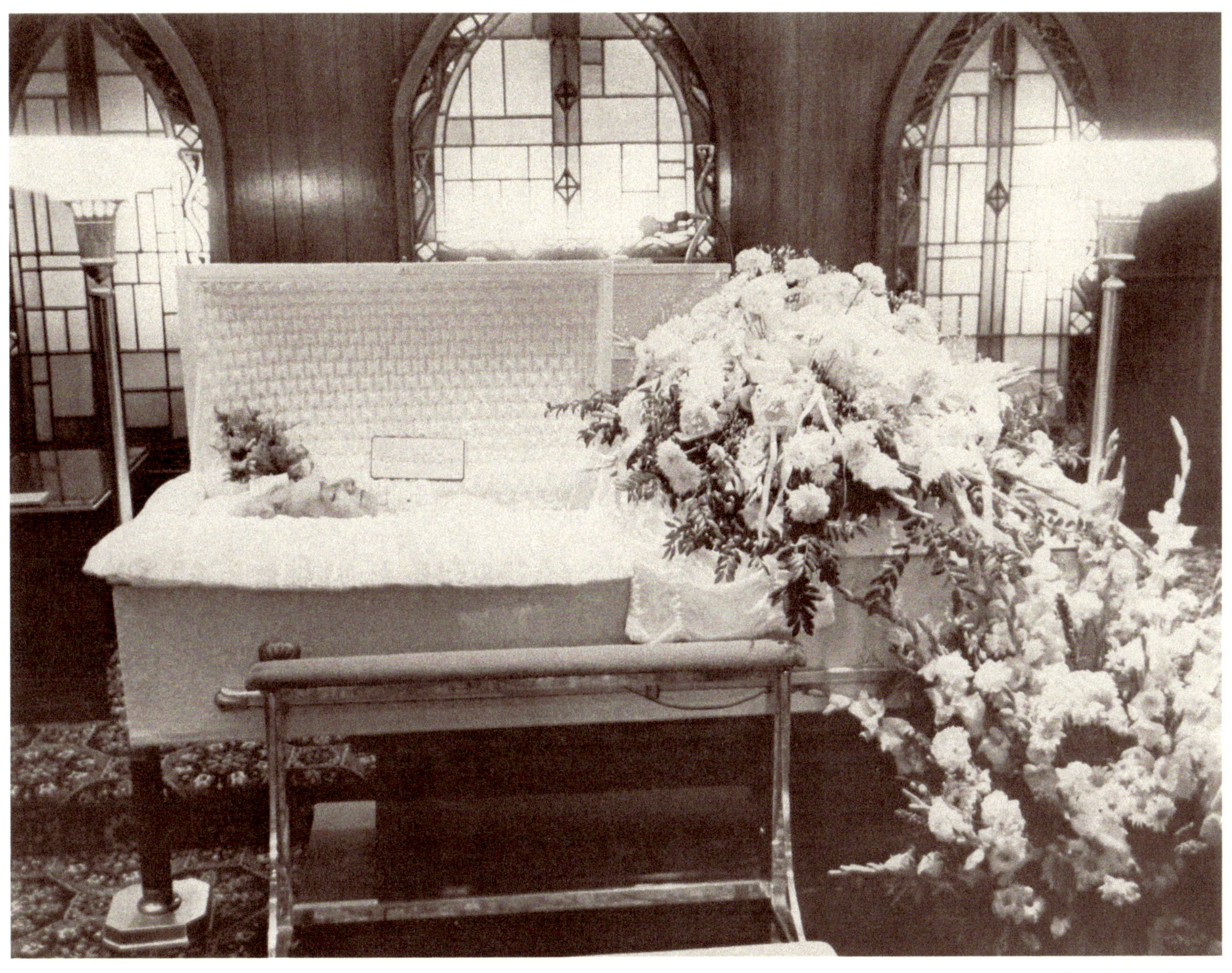

Photo by Frank Stewart

This interior of my mind
Where a scorpion has stung me
So many times I refuse to die
Because I love you and resist all
Poison in my flesh.
Hold me, scold me.
I will suffer less.
Are you my scorpion
Or my champion?

They lean over me and say:
"Who deathed you who,
who, who, who, who. . . .
I whisper: "Tell you presently. . .
Shortly. . . this evening. . . .
Tomorrow. . ."
Tomorrow is here
And you out there safe.
I'm safe in here, Tootsie.

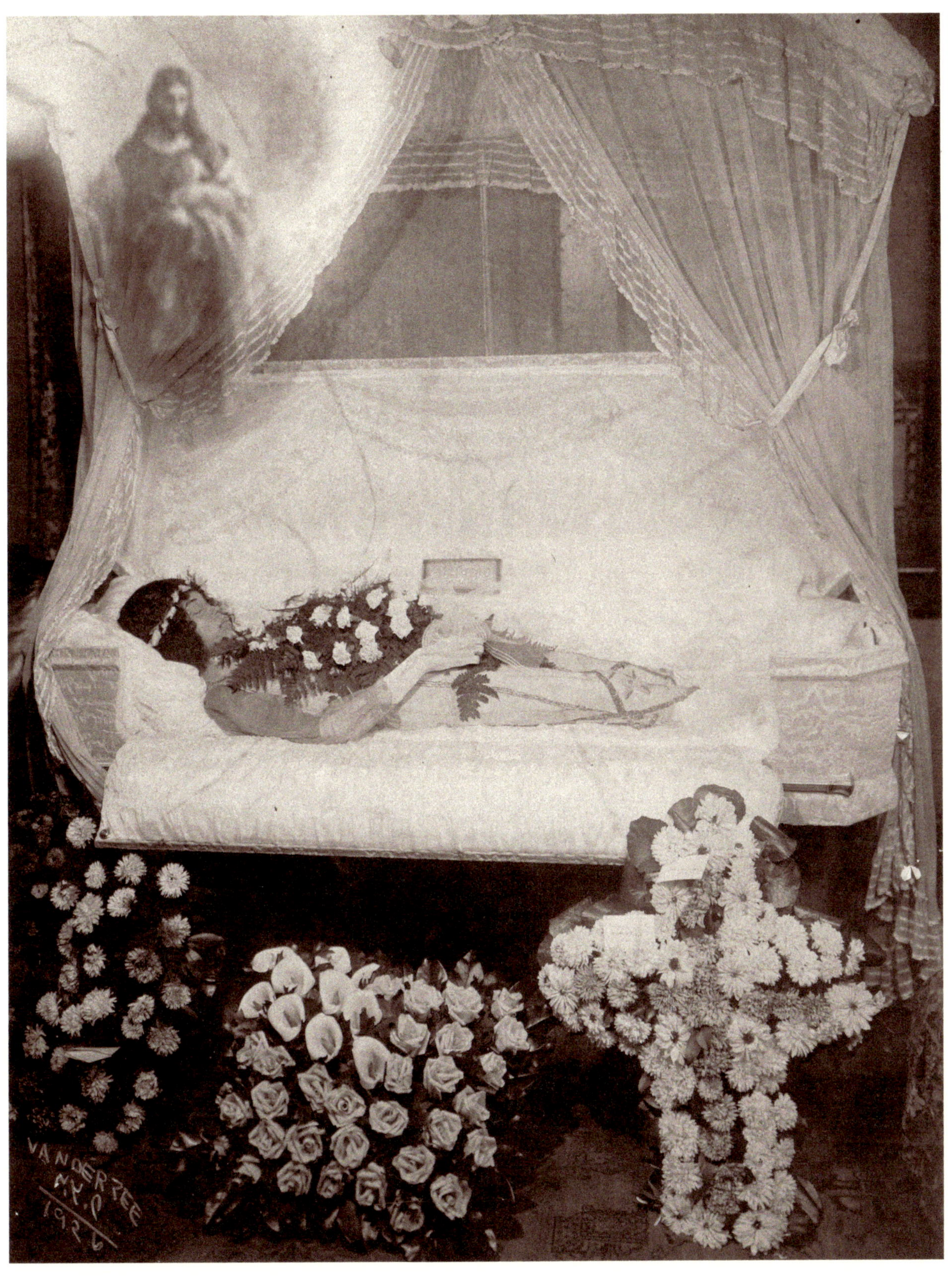
VANDERZEE
N.Y.C.
1926

Done crossed every river,
Done reached this one;
Now I know my crossin's done.
Hallelujah, Lord, your rest feel good.
Hallelujah, Lord, your rest feel good.

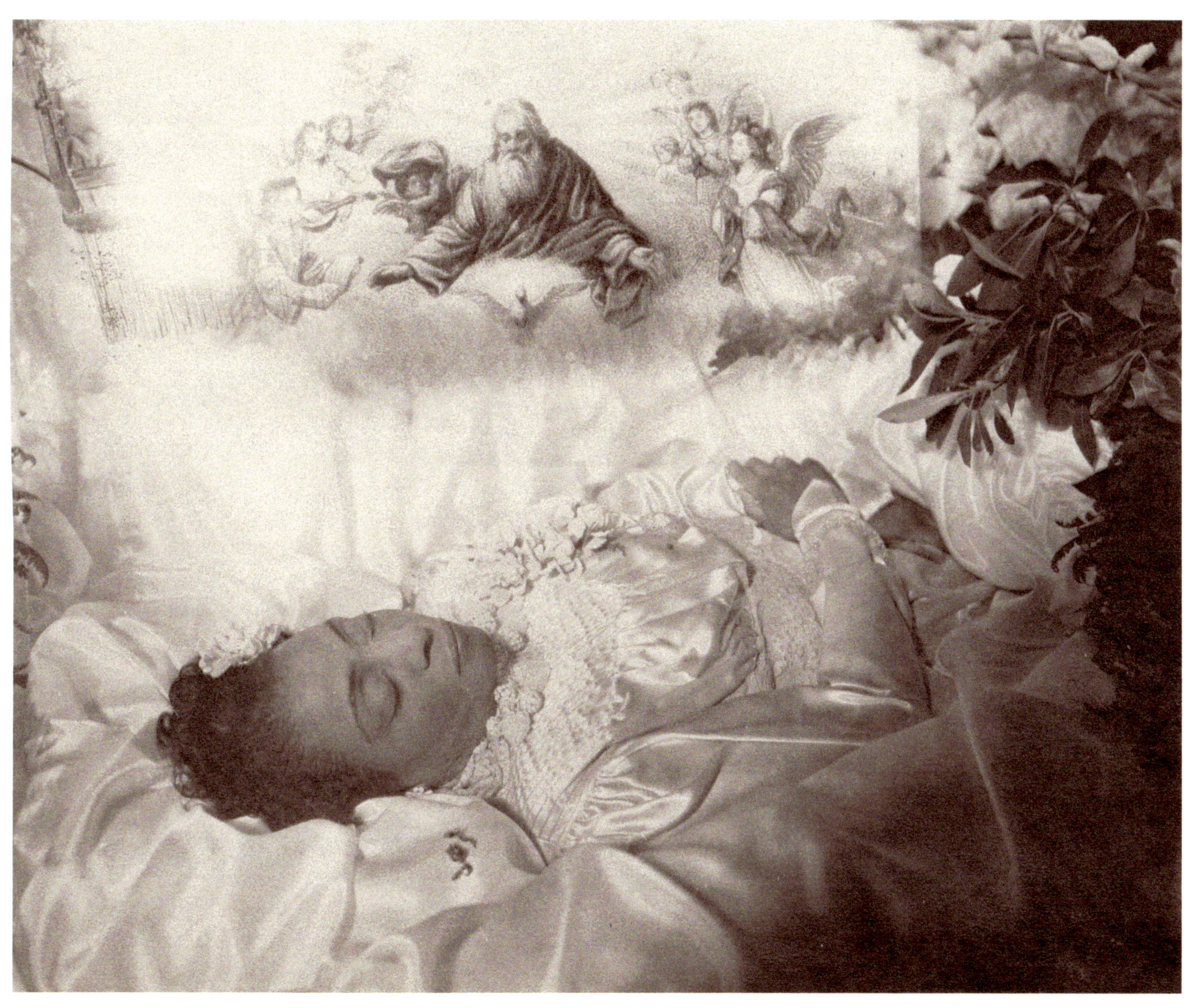

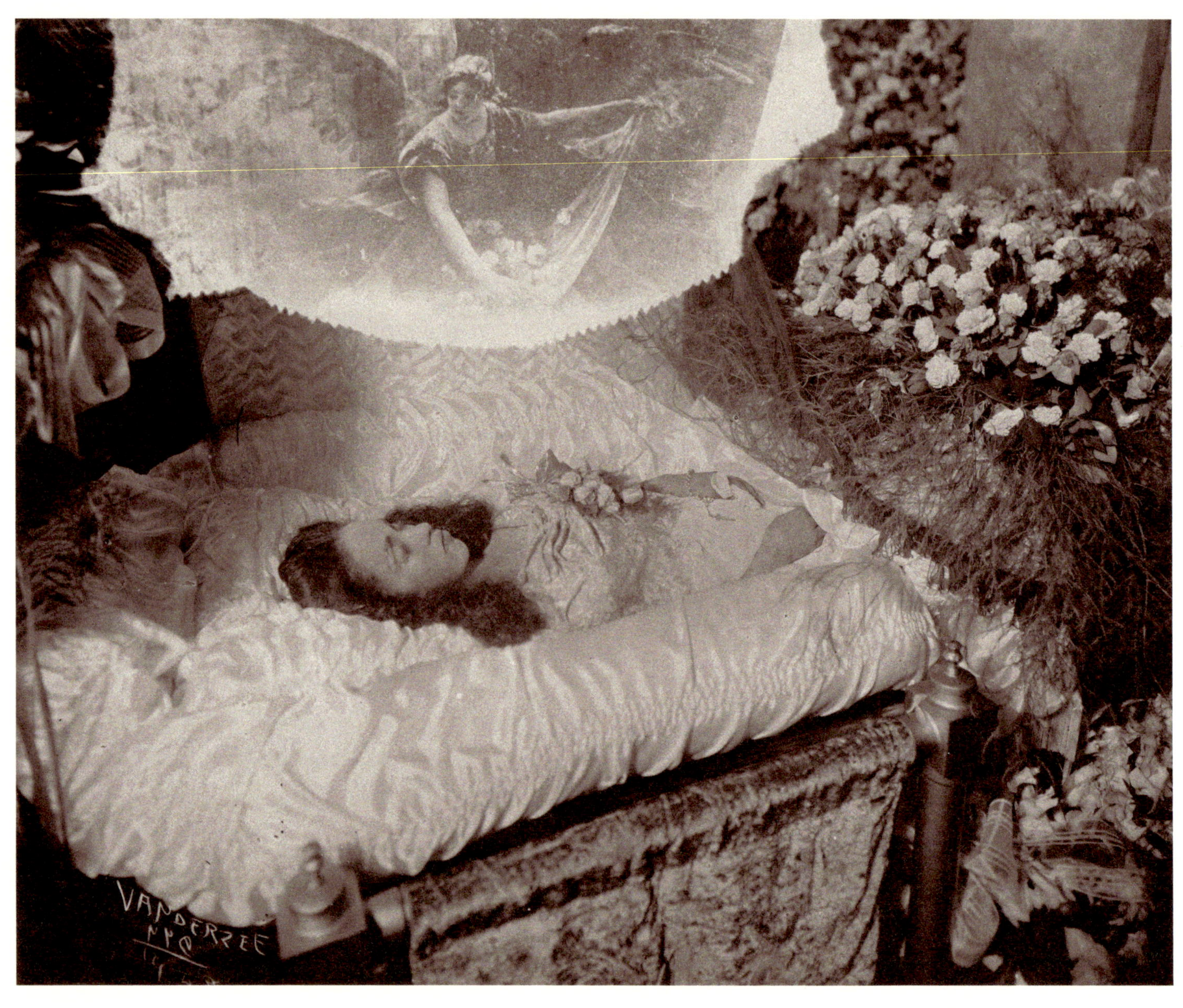
VANDERZEE
NYC

I had a river in my mind
Where I had drowned myself
So many times I felt sharp flesh
Of water underneath
My eyelids; and between my toes
The minnows smuggle time
To hoard it where all shells begin
To grow what children on the shore
Have always begged to listen to.

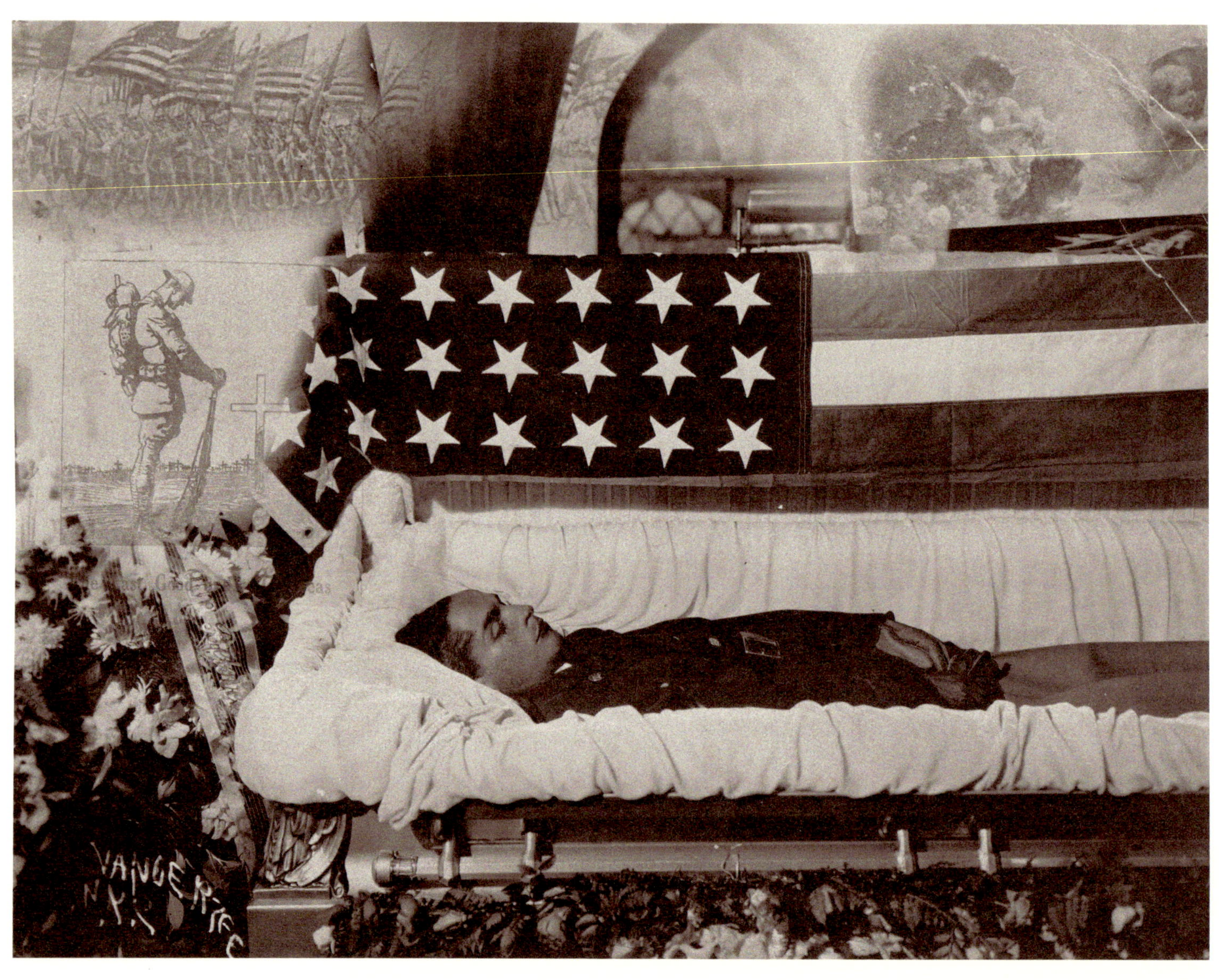

Soldiers

MR. VAN DER ZEE, WERE THE SOLDIERS OF THE 369th REGIMENT THE ONES WHO WENT TO PARIS?

Yes, they were "The Bronze Men." I photographed some of those men that were in that army. (This was the one Kate wanted to put me in.) I've got pictures of Roberts and Johnson, the first two that were decorated for bravery. There were quite a few of them. When they went over there, they were supposed to be American soldiers, but they wouldn't let them fight with the American Army. They put them in the French Army. It's because they hadn't integrated them with the other white American soldiers. The French Army had a lot of those African soldiers in it, too. My sister painted a picture of one of these African soldiers, with a bayonet in his hand, standing over a German soldier. You know, he looked more surprised by that black face than he was by the predicament he was in. There may have been other contingents, other than the 369th, which was when I started makin' pictures up there at the armory of the fellows that were gettin' ready to go, but I don't know of them. I also photographed some of them that came back. Written in one of the books of Colonel Heywood, who was head of "The 369th," were accounts of bravery of the black men that served in his regiment. One boy came back who had been wounded three hundred and sixty times with shrapnel. In fact, he lost one leg over there.

DID ANY OF THEM WHO HAD LOST AN ARM OR LEG EVER GET THEIR PICTURE TAKEN?

I don't remember, but I did make some pictures of some of those who had come back with dishonorable discharges. In those days that particular discharge was colored yellow. I wondered why they wanted them [the pictures].

WHY WERE THE DISCHARGE PAPERS YELLOW?

Dishonorable.

WERE THE MEN COWARDS?

Well, a whole lot of them went over there that didn't believe in fighting anyhow.

WAS IT PARTICULARLY SAD TO PHOTOGRAPH YOUNG SOLDIERS?

Not that I can recall. I made one of a fella, he wasn't a soldier, tried to hold up the subway with an artificial gun; he was shot. I made a picture of him in the casket at Turner's Funeral Parlor.

WHAT DID YOU FEEL ABOUT THAT?

I thought he had made a mistake.

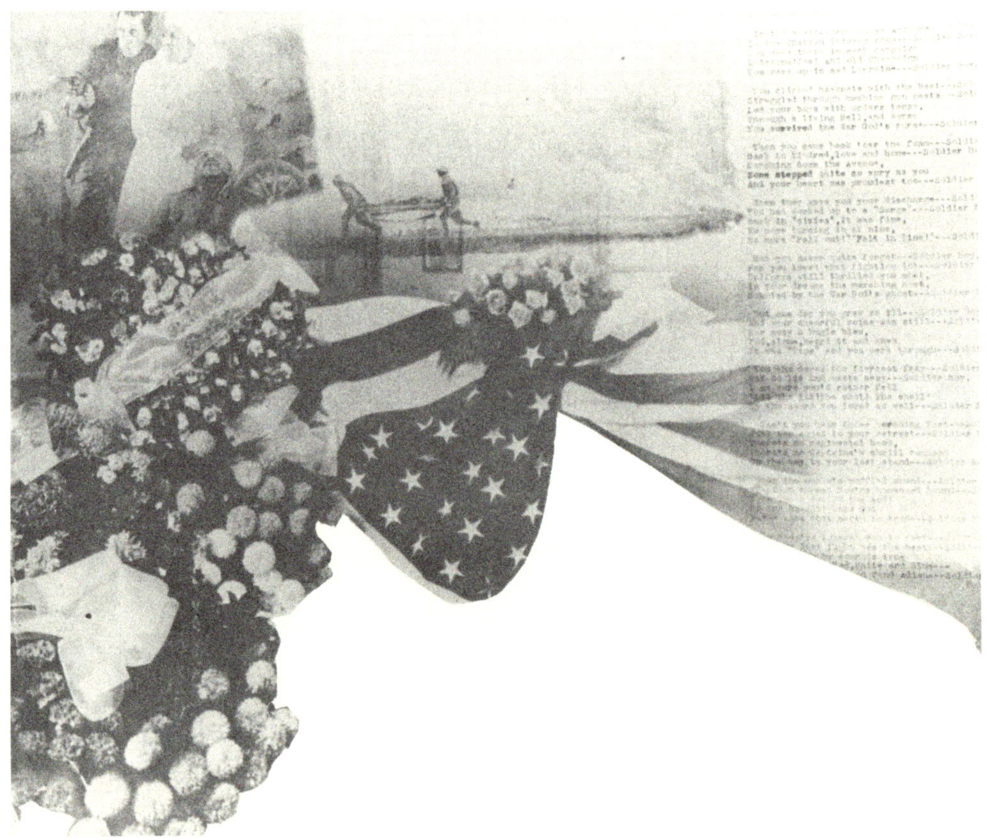

War Games

Who presides over our pieces
of death:
We had our fertility shot out
In the Marne, Verdun, Okinawa, Viet Nam
Or places we couldn't pro-
nounce
Only with shots of heroin or booze.
My God, who from Hell was
appointed to shred
Us piecemeal war by eternal
war
Like meat grinders to our souls?
We wanted the sun to shine
on our cufflinks,
On our children, into our hair,
Not on medals, or uniform buttons.
We will not even permit you
To look on us dead wherever
we lie
In muddy waters or dry soil or
hitched in air.
If miracles try to resurrect us
We'll only be ground in the
grinders again.
We cannot trust—Amen.

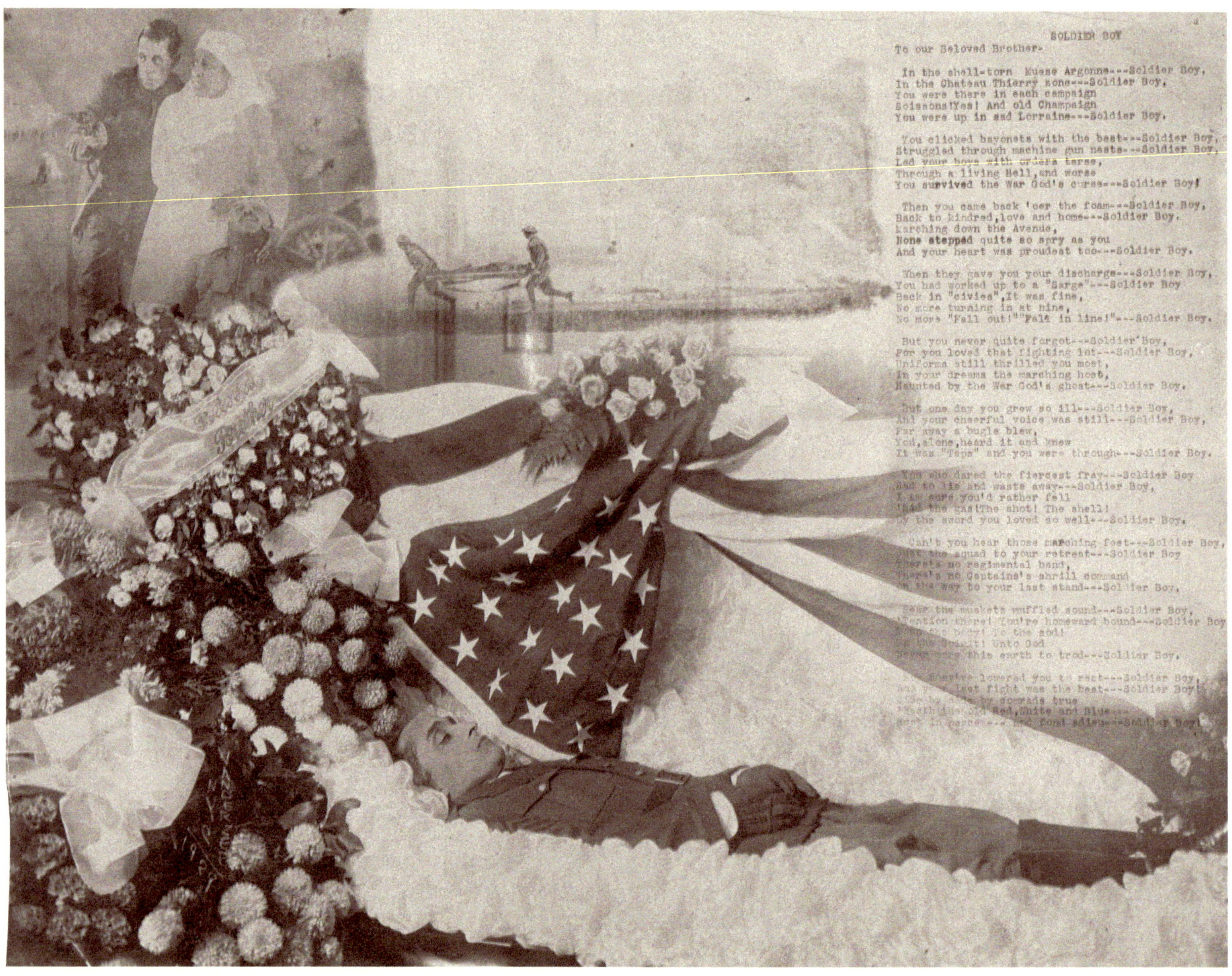
SOLDIER BOY
To our Beloved Brother-
In the shell-torn Muese Argonne---Soldier Boy,
In the Chateau Thierry zone---Soldier Boy,
You were there in each campaign
Soissons!Yes! And old Champaign
You were up in sad Lorraine---Soldier Boy.
You clicked bayonets with the best---Soldier Boy,
Struggled through machine gun nests---Soldier Boy,
Led your boys with orders terse,
Through a living Hell,and worse
You survived the War God's curse---Soldier Boy!
Then you came back 'oer the foam---Soldier Boy,
Back to kindred,love and home---Soldier Boy.
Marching down the Avenue,
None stepped quite so spry as you
And your heart was proudest too---Soldier Boy.
When they gave you your discharge---Soldier Boy,
You had worked up to a "Sarge"---Soldier Boy
Back in "civies",It was fine,
No more turning in at nine,
No more "Fall out!""Fall in line!"---Soldier Boy.
But you never quite forgot---Soldier Boy,
For you loved that fighting lot---Soldier Boy,
Uniforms still thrilled you most,
In your dreams the marching host,
Haunted by the War God's ghost---Soldier Boy.
But one day you grew so ill---Soldier Boy,
And your cheerful voice was still---Soldier Boy,
Far away a bugle blew,
You,alone,heard it and knew
It was "Taps" and you were through---Soldier Boy.
You who dared the fiercest fray---Soldier Boy
Had to lie and waste away---Soldier Boy,
you'd rather fell
The shot! The shell!
the sword you loved so well---Soldier Boy.
Can't you hear those marching feet---Soldier Boy,
squad to your retreat---Soldier Boy
no regimental band,
Captains's shrill command
to your last stand---Soldier Boy.
the muskets muffled sound---Soldier Boy,
You're homeward bound---Soldier Boy
to the sod!
Unto God
this earth to trod---Soldier Boy.
lowered you to rest---Soldier Boy,
last fight was the best---Soldier Boy!
by comrade true
Red,White and Blue--

I loved life like a budding broad
I never had the nerve to kiss.
Take back your medals,
Stamp on the stars,
Then cry for me,
Please anybody cry for me.
Lick my dead wounds,
You mothers!

Mourners & the Posing of the Dead

IN MOST OF THE PHOTOGRAPHS THAT I'VE SEEN OF THE DEAD, THE MOURNERS APPEAR TO BE SOLEMN AND SERIOUS. YET SHOULDN'T WE REJOICE WHEN, AS YOU SAY, A SOUL GOES TO GOD? WHY DIDN'T THE MOURNERS SMILE IN SOME OF THE PICTURES?

I guess they didn't smile because it would look like a joke. I did have some of the mothers and fathers smile, when they posed with their dead children, for the "last" picture. But that seemed to be different. It's as the man said when he was dying, he said, "My tears are not of joy, but of sorrow." He said he hated to go because he was sorry that he couldn't take them along.

THESE PEOPLE DON'T LOOK AS IF THEY WANT TO GO, EITHER.

No, there's very few of them that do. There's been some of them that did want to get in the casket with them and go along with them.

DID YOU EVER SEE ANYBODY TRY TO GET IN THE CASKET?

No, I didn't see them, because as I said, they always have the undertaker and so forth to control them.

HAVE YOU EVER SEEN ANYBODY TRY TO JUMP INTO A GRAVE?

I've heard some of them take the body there to the undertaker's and they'd not be exactly dead but in a coma or somethin', and then the

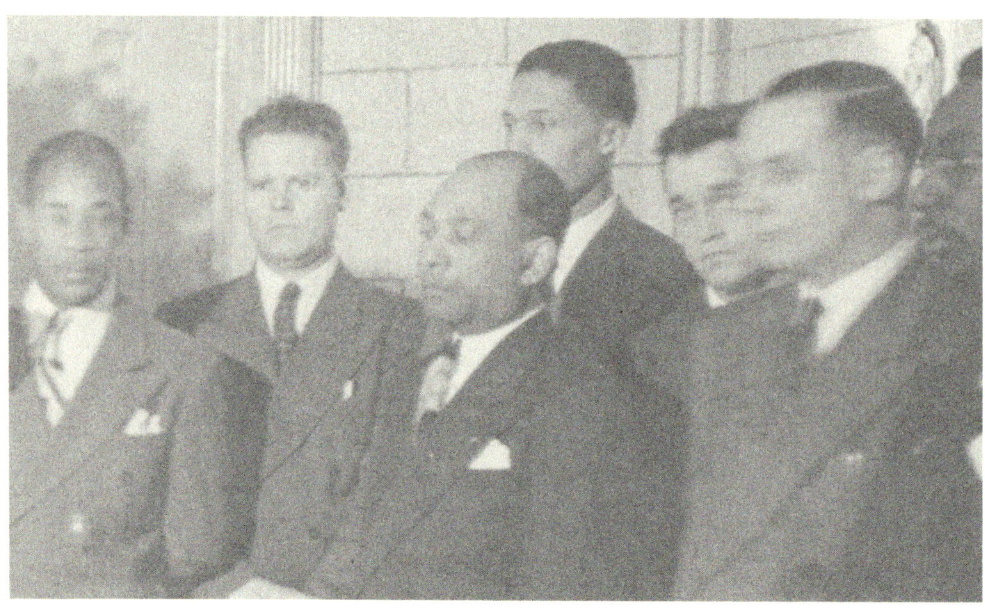

body would sit up and the undertaker would take to the window. Yeah, he took to the window.

OH, DO YOU THINK THAT THESE DEAD FOLKS INDEED SAT UP?

Years ago, when they didn't embalm them, why, then it was different. Sometimes they buried them even though they wasn't even dead.

AT WHAT POINT, IF YOU REMEMBER, DID PEOPLE STOP POSING WITH THE DEAD?

I didn't know they had stopped. They're still doing it today. Sometimes the family wanted to be there to show the other relatives just how the deceased had been put away.

DID YOU EVER SEE THE DEAD WITH A PRONOUNCED SMILE ON THEIR FACE?

Some undertakers are more capable of doin' that than others. They could shape the face up so's to make it look more like a smile and so forth. But the majority of them, they just smooth the face up. Sometimes they'd put cotton in there, to fill it out.

DID YOU EVER HEAR OF ANY CASES WHERE PEOPLE POSED THE DEAD WITH THEIR EYES OPEN?

No, they almost always close the eyes.

WHY DO THEY DO THAT, DO YOU KNOW?

Well, do you want to see them layin' there with their eyes open? You know, some of them did die with their eyes open, but the undertaker would close them. Long time ago they used to close them by putting

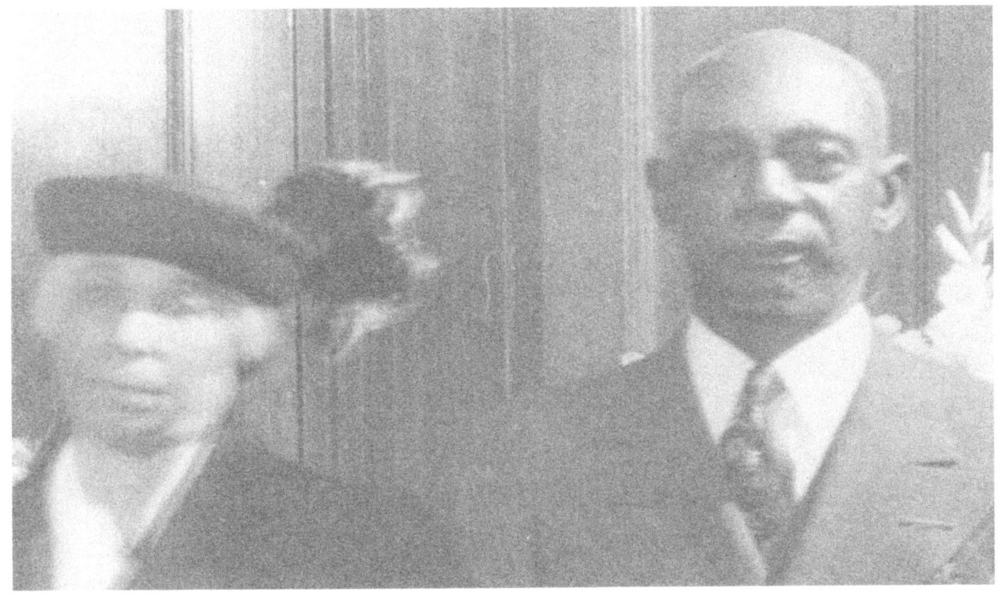

pennies on the eyelids of the deceased. That's where the saying comes from: "He'd steal the pennies off a dead man's eyes."

IF THE UNDERTAKER IS TRYING TO GIVE A LIFELIKE APPEARANCE, WOULDN'T OPENING THE EYES AND MAKING THE MOUTH SMILE BE MORE LOGICAL THAN GIVING THE "JUST FALLEN ASLEEP" LOOK?

Who'd want all that? You would think they weren't dead.

BUT ISN'T THAT WHAT YOU ATTEMPTED TO DO BY PLACING THE NEWSPAPER IN THE DEAD MAN'S HAND? WHY DIDN'T THE UNDERTAKER GO ONE STEP FURTHER AND OPEN HIS EYES AS IF HE WERE READING?

Well, when we made them that way, they were usually alive. Had a little more life and everything.

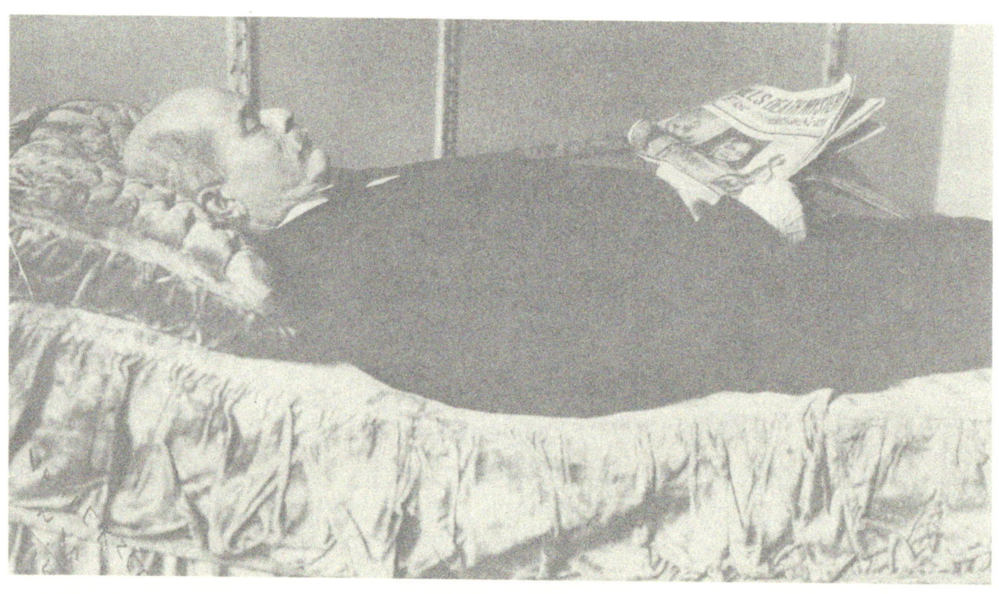

The Congregation

Receive us with the despairing pimples
On our faces:
Our popped-up pussy dreams.
We will be the good-byes never said,
The farewells fortunetellers never glimpse.
All our farewells cry to thee,
Hammer on thy house!
A hail of farewells!
Are you awake
With your eyes shut?

Man is the Head of Everything Big on Earth

God is the three-in-one, the Father, the Son, and the Holy Ghost. Christ was made in the image of Man to come down, I guess, because He went through the tortures and routine of men on earth. But He, His Father sent Him to do that. No man has ever seen God. The Bible also says that "We shall see Him face to face."

WHO FACE TO FACE?

The Lord. We shall see Him face to face. He was made in the image of man. On account of the wonders that He's performed and the big duties that He has to perform, to make the world and everything in it.

AND YOU FEEL THAT MAYBE THAT'S WHAT MEN DO?

That's the thing to be expected. And He made Adam, and He said that it was not good for man to be alone. So He took one of Adam's ribs, and from that He made the woman.

WHY DO YOU KEEP SAYING "HE"? DO YOU THINK GOD IS MALE?

Well, since you've asked me that, I'll try to think why. I guess, 'cause man is the head of every big thing here on earth, naturally he thought that God was a man too, but a more powerful one than these earthly men. But He's always been pictured as a man. Christ, when He was on earth, He said, "In my Father's house, there are many mansions. I go to prepare a place for you. And when I go, I will return to receive you. And none go to my Father's house except through me."

WHO WROTE THAT?

One of the prophets. They were chosen by the Lord to write those things. Their hands was guided by the Lord. He picked out certain ones to write those things. Some of 'em didn't want to write it, but they was picked, chosen by the Lord to write it. They were Matthew, Mark, Luke, and John.

ALL MEN, RIGHT?
Yeah.

SUPPOSE TOMORROW YOU FOUND OUT THAT GOD WAS NOT MALE?

He wouldn't be a Father if He wasn't male.

HE WOULD BE A MOTHER. GOD THE MOTHER.

It's one of them same things. Which came first, the chicken or the egg? "He" has always been.

YOU WOULD HAVE TO SAY, "IN MY MOTHER'S HOUSE THERE ARE MANY MANSIONS."

But the Bible doesn't say that. As I said before, lots of things I've taken for granted and I never questioned it myself. Although I was brought up in the Episcopal Church, where we always went to Sunday School, I never saw a picture that showed God as a woman. But then these are quotations that have already been written. They probably would be changed by the present leaders of today.

WHAT OTHER QUOTATIONS DO YOU LIKE?

Now, here's one that helped me, "After toil, comes rest," and you see, I've rested.

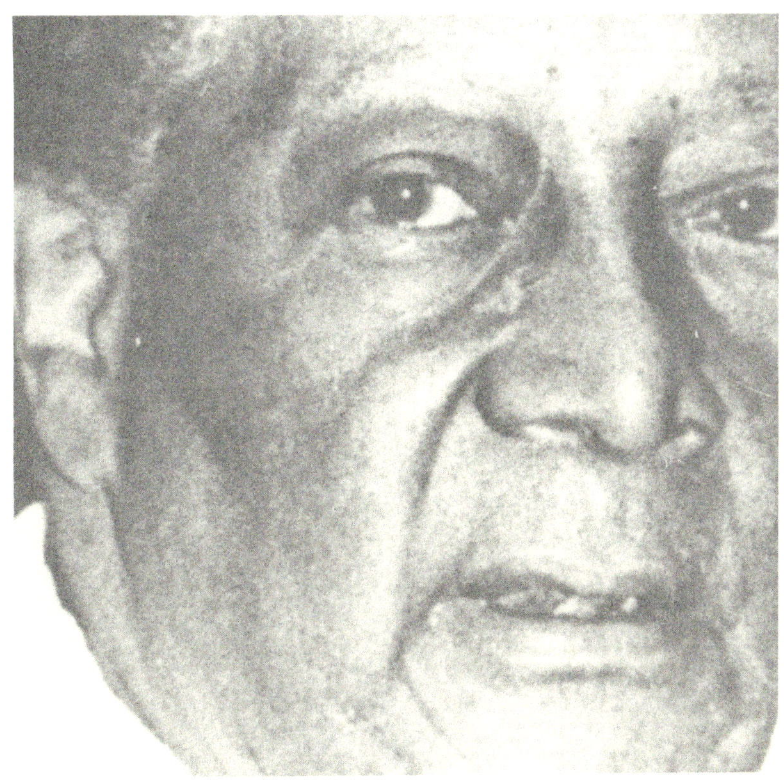

WHEN A PERSON DIES, WHY ARE THEY THOUGHT TO BE AT REST?

The body's at rest, but we don't know what goes on after that.

THE BODY'S NOT AT REST, IT'S AT ROT.

They say the soul and the life leave the body, and after that it's "dust thou art and to dust returneth." You can kill the body, but you can't kill the soul.

DO YOU BELIEVE THAT THE SOUL GOES SOMEPLACE ELSE AND PASSES INTO OTHER FORMS OF LIFE?

Everything is possible with God.

MR. VAN DER ZEE, WHAT ABOUT THOSE BODIES WITH PIECES OF FINGERS HERE AND PIECES OF BRAIN THERE, WITH A HAND OR SOMETHING LEFT OUT ON THE HIGHWAY? IT SEEMS TO ME THAT THE RESURRECTION OF THE BODY, SUCH AS YOU CONCEIVE OF, IS LIKE TRYING TO FIND A HARLEM APARTMENT AFTER THE BUILDING HAS FALLEN DOWN.

(At this point, Mr. Van Der Zee reverses his stand.)

What about those that have been cremated? That's what I've often said, I've said, when the Judgement Day comes, these guys that have been cremated, whose ashes have been scattered to the wind, gonna have an awful time tryin' to get their hind parts together.

DID YOU EVER SEE PEOPLE PLACE OBJECTS IN THE COFFIN ALONG WITH THE DEAD?

I've seen them put religious objects in there, but nothing else. I do know that the Chinese bring hot food there and put it on the grave. There was this guy who was at the next grave one time who said, "When do you think your friend's comin' up and eat that stuff you got there?" The Chinese man said, "He'll come. He'll come same time your friend comes up and smells the flowers you put on there."

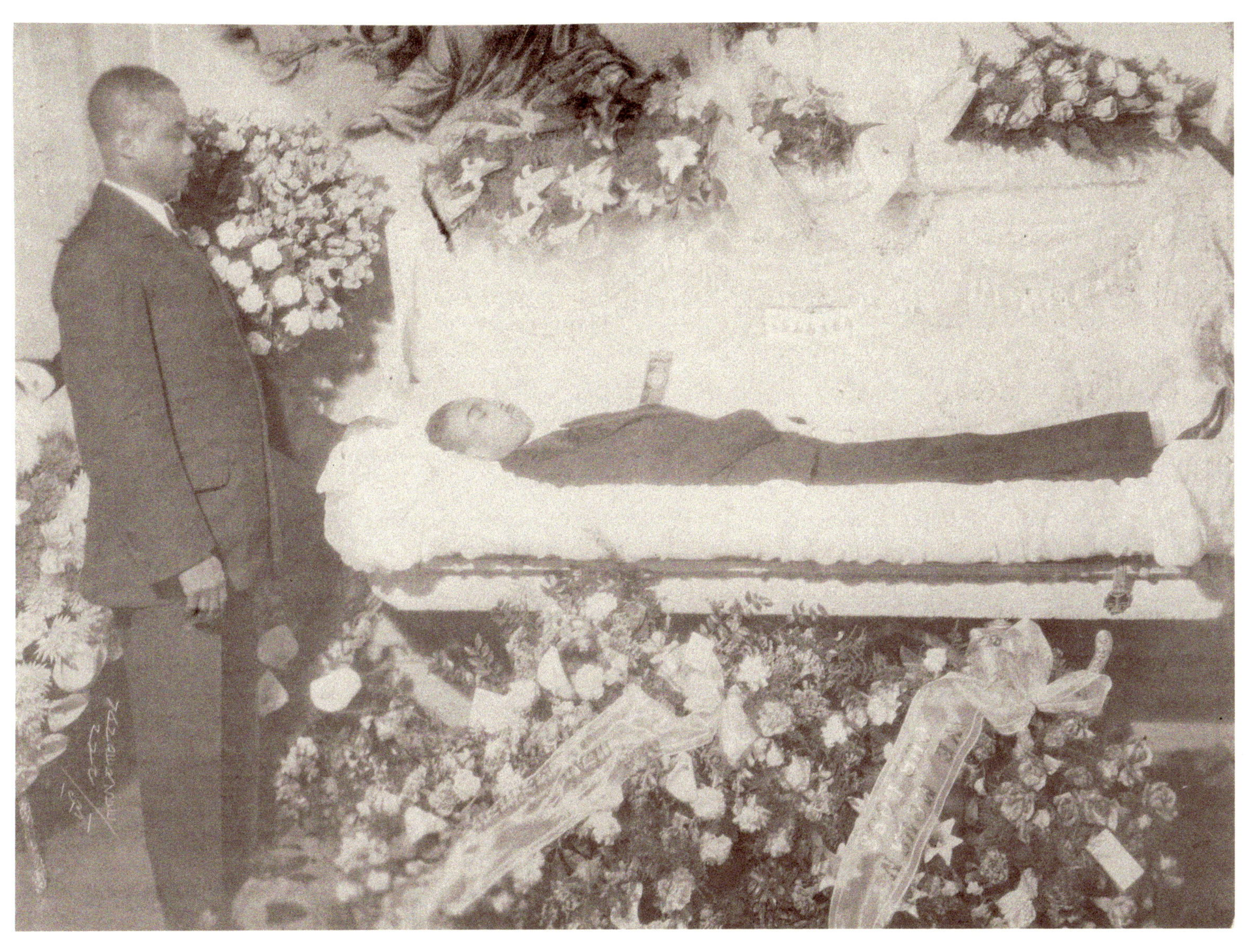

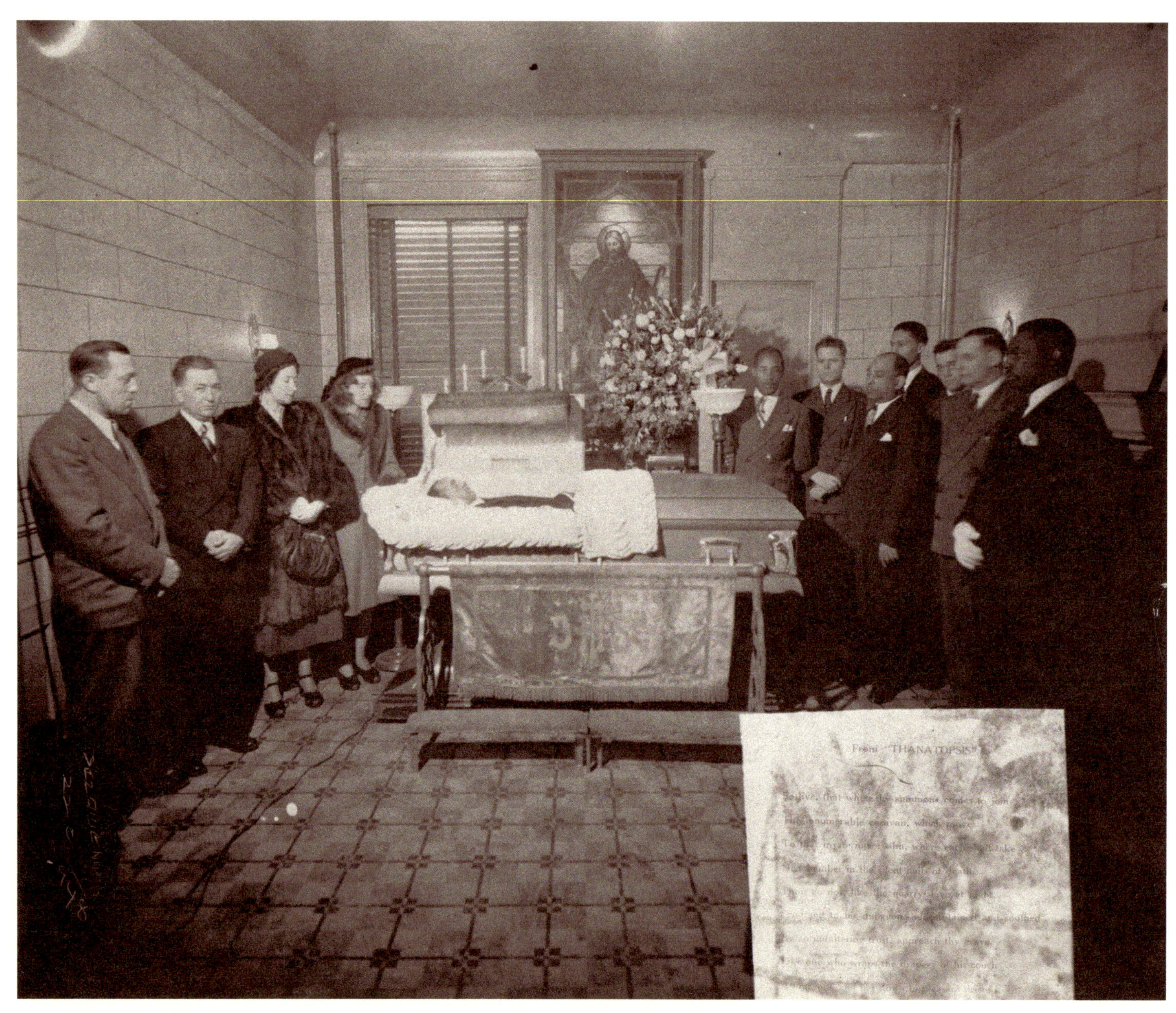
From "THANATOPSIS"

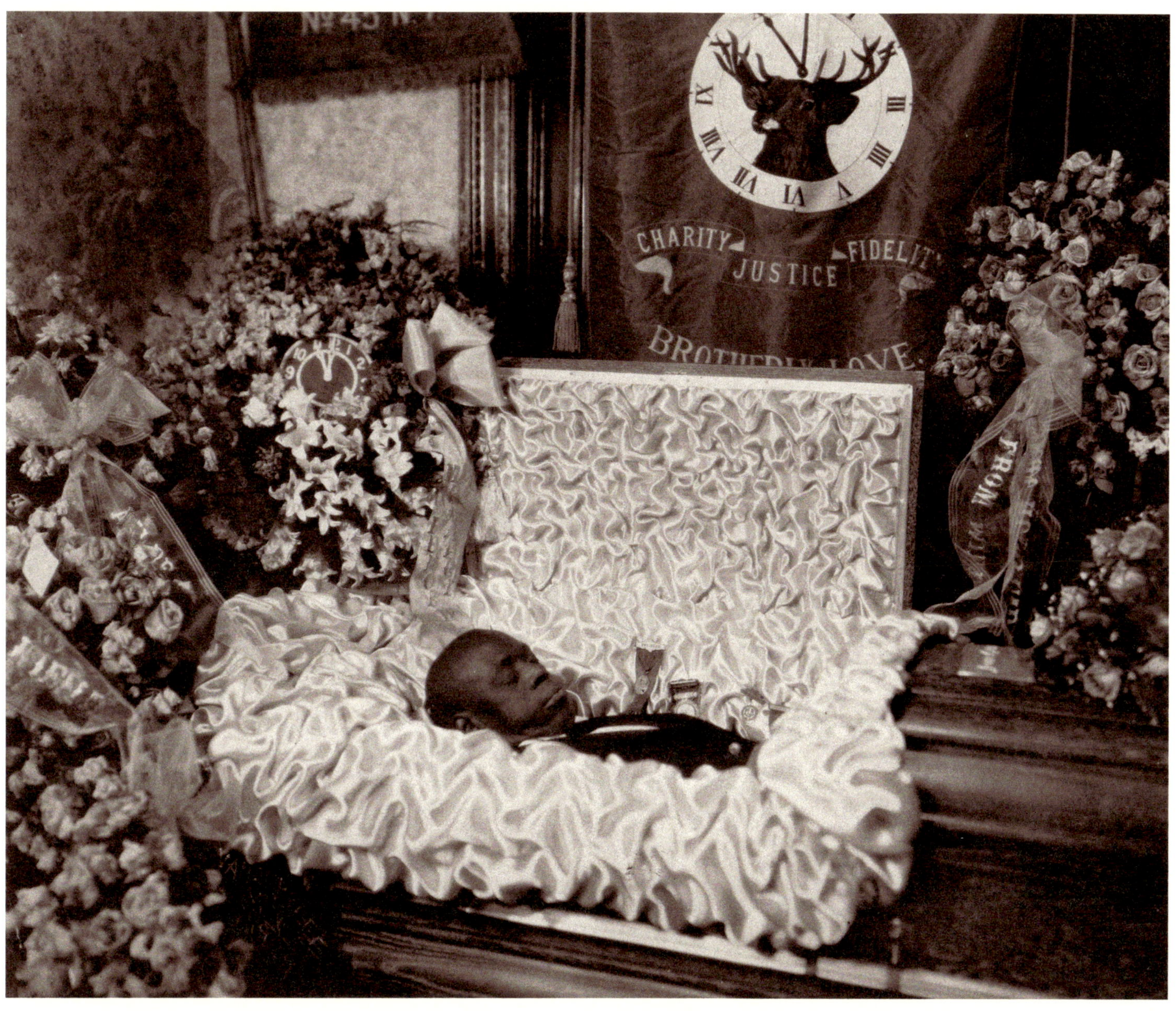

I thought when I died,
I would be dead,
But worms are after the tongue
I preached salvation with.
You'd think they would've waited
Till I was in the dirt
And my flowers dead.

They been waitin' here
Since I was born, I reckon.
I won't be nowhere near whole
On resurrection day
To join the hosts.

The carried-out box
(pallbearers gloves:
Are the cheapest there are)
Clothing the stuffed dead
Happens to us
With our veils,
Our tears,
Our flowers, food,
The hearses that are elegant,
The singing that kills the flowers.

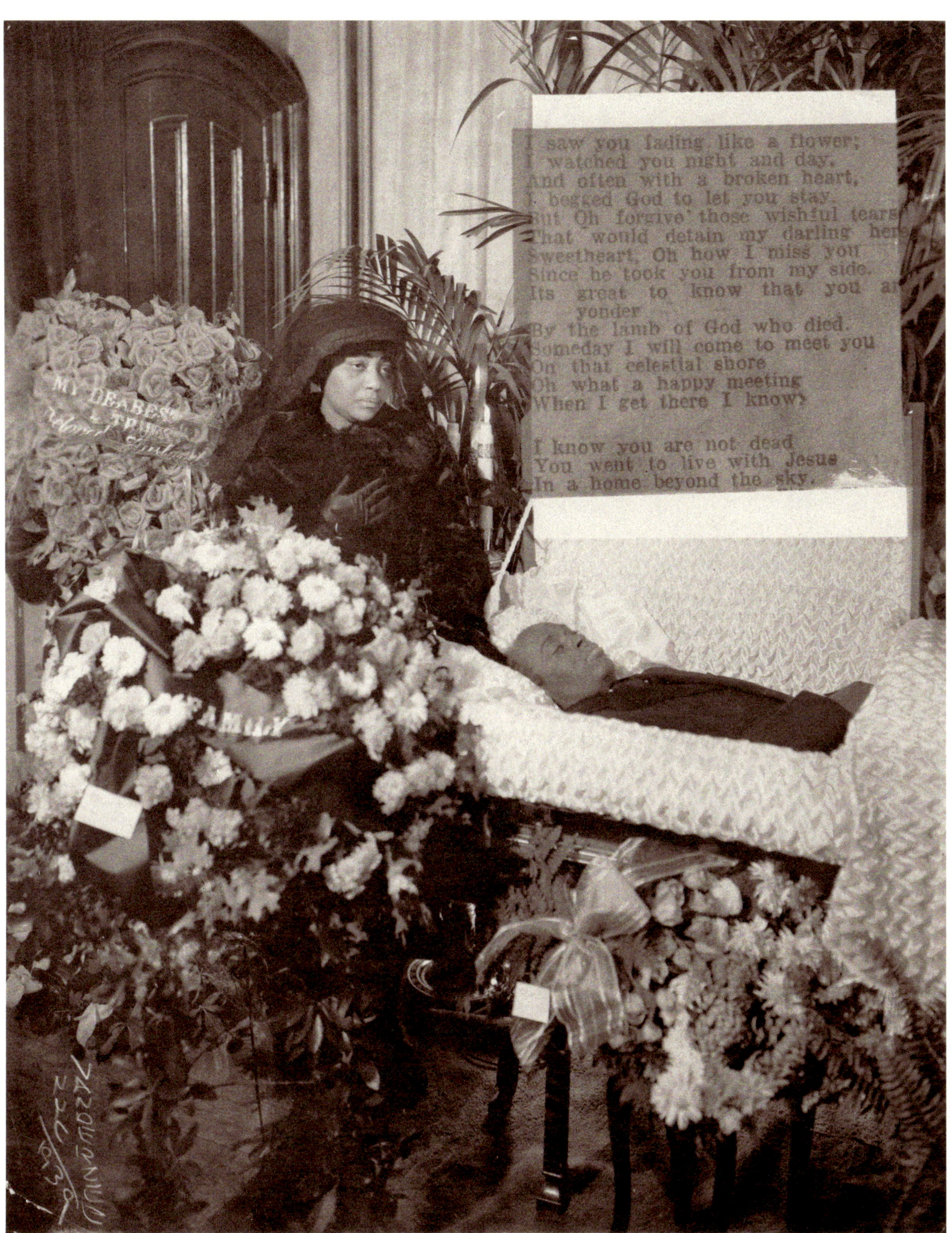
I saw you fading like a flower;
I watched you night and day.
And often with a broken heart,
I begged God to let you stay.
But Oh forgive those wishful tears
That would detain my darling her
Sweetheart, Oh how I miss you
Since he took you from my side.
Its great to know that you ar
yonder
By the lamb of God who died.
Someday I will come to meet you
On that celestial shore
Oh what a happy meeting
When I get there I know.
I know you are not dead
You went to live with Jesus
In a home beyond the sky.
FAMILY

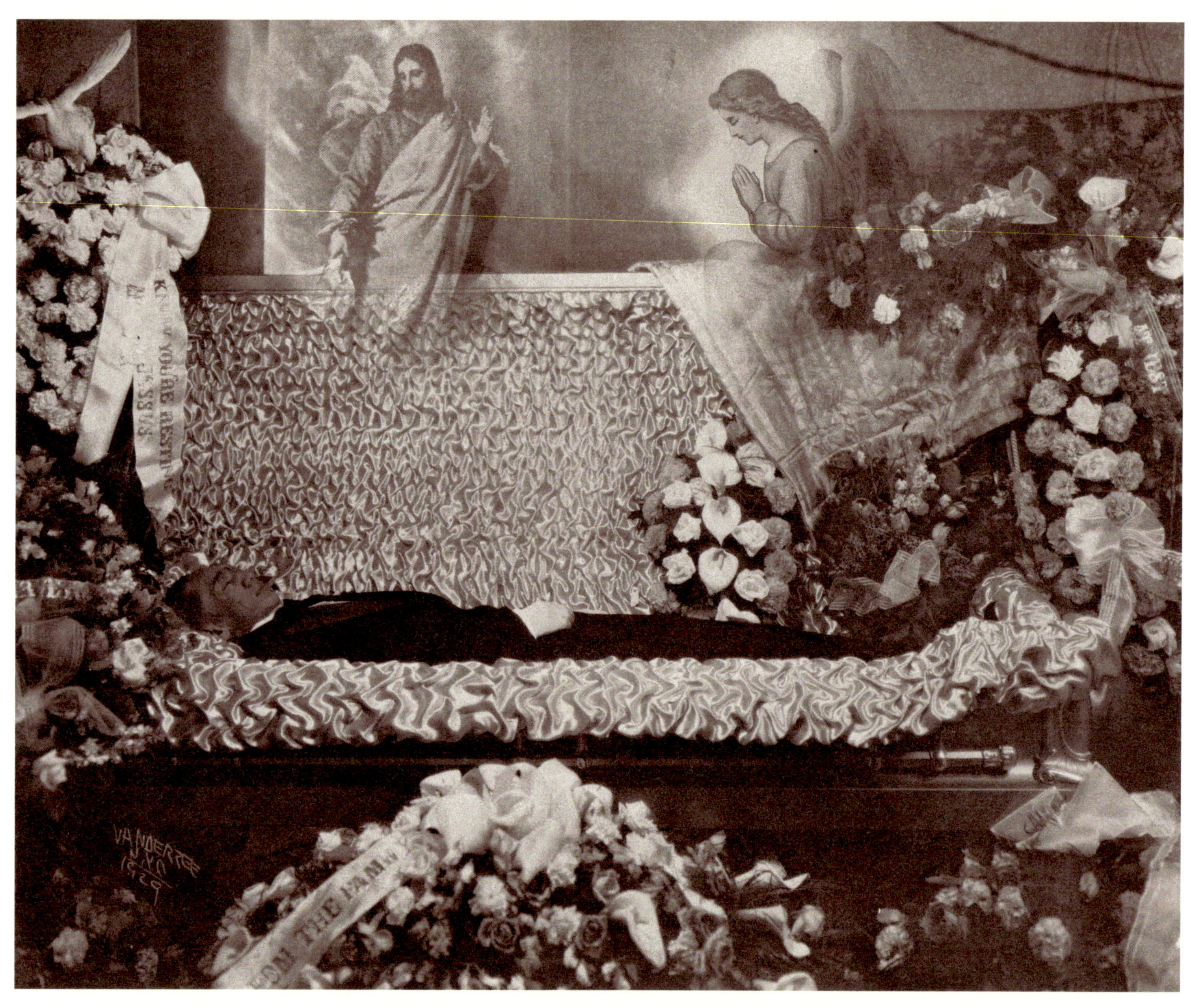
YOU'RE RESTING
VANDERZEE
N.Y.C.
1929

Undertaker say:
"This casket's right pretty,
Satin everywhere.
You can't do better
Even at the cut-rate.
Only cost 541 smackers
With the key to lock it up
And the brass plate
To identify on that morning."
"Chile, we played 541
And won.
And here you is!"
"Yes, here I is."

We grew so far away from each other
And got lonesome. Please was
Our only vocabulary.
Now and again: Will you be with me please.
A word with a vegetable sound:
Please…

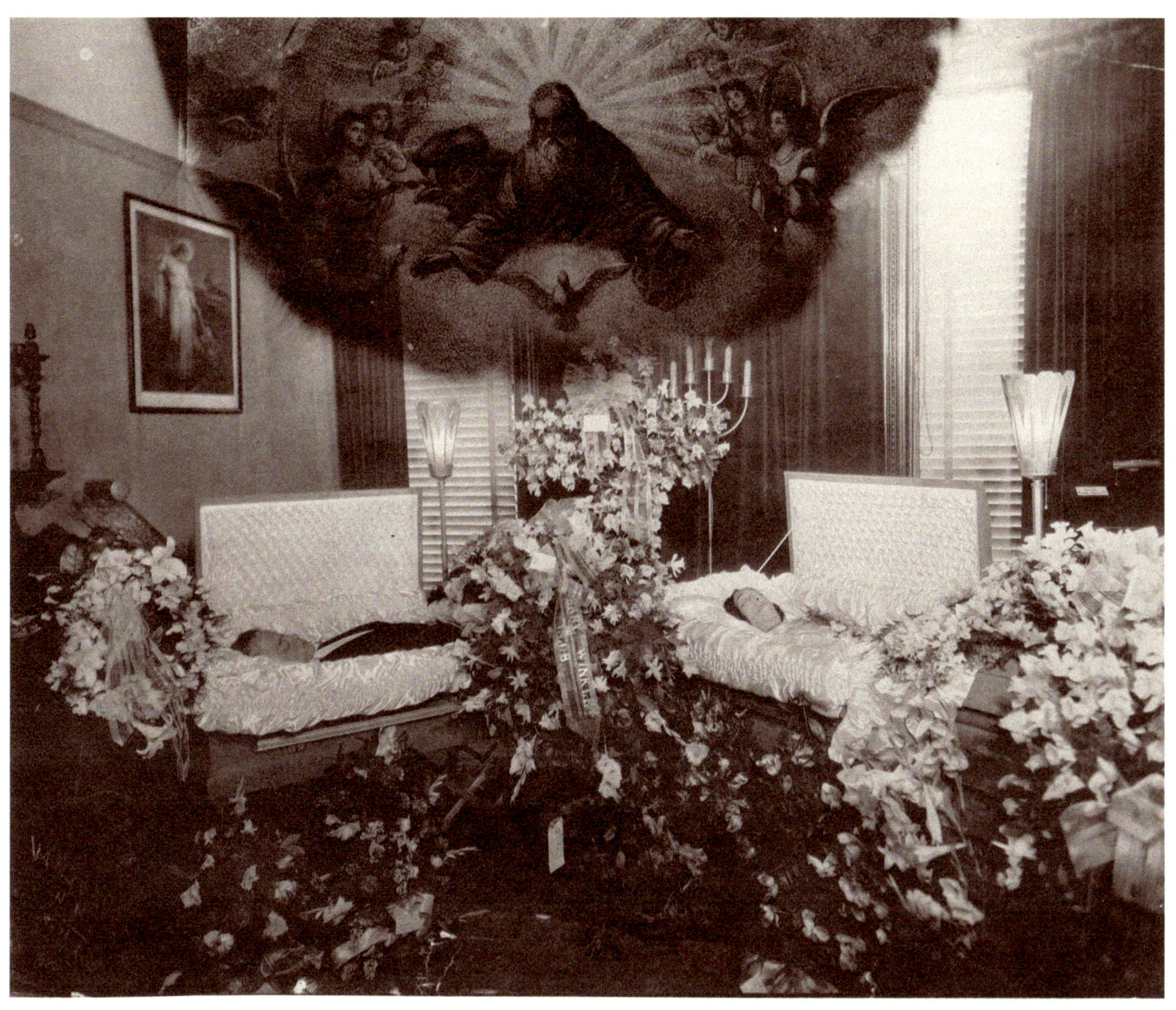

HOW DO YOU SEE DEATH, MR. VAN DER ZEE?

So when one more clean shirt lasts me the rest of time. When I pass out on this long last journey that I shall ever make and I cease to soothe with soft words and song a heart in which there is an ache, I trust that tears will dim few eyes and those who do weep will soon forget.

(At this point, Mr. Van Der Zee lights up his cigar.)

The Pastor

Be it resolved resolved resolved resolved:
Oh let it be the wheel of resurrection
Upturning blooming waters from their souls:
Oh let them splash flat-vertical and high
To arc a rainbow in that triumph time
When startled angels graduate, cum laude,
From adoration to the bright divine:
The indescribable, the only All.
Watch wisely for Jerusalem, my dears,
And every bleeding lamb from Ararat.

Description of Plates

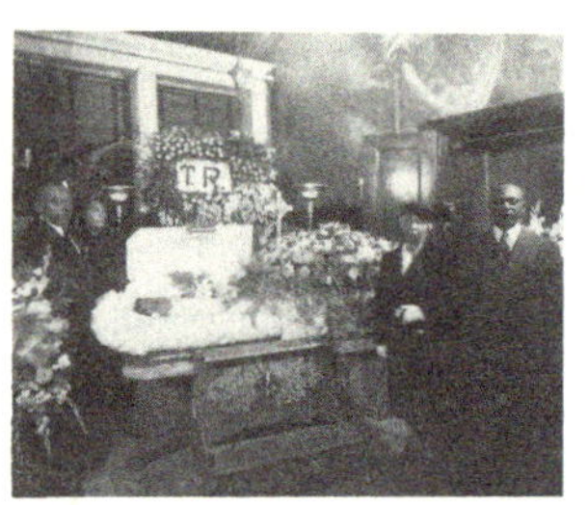

DID YOU TAKE MORE PICTURES OF OLDER WOMEN THAN YOU DID OF ANYONE ELSE?

Well it didn't seem like that they were so old at the time.

DID YOU EVER FEEL THAT PHOTOGRAPHING FUNERALS WAS MORBID?

It was all in the course of the work, but some of these autopsy cases were sort of nauseating, where you had to photograph the insides.

WHY DID YOU PUT INSERTS INTO YOUR PHOTOGRAPHS?

Well I just put them in to take away the gruesomeness of the picture, to make it look more like "suffering little children come unto me and I'll give you rest." In some cases I put in Biblical scriptures."

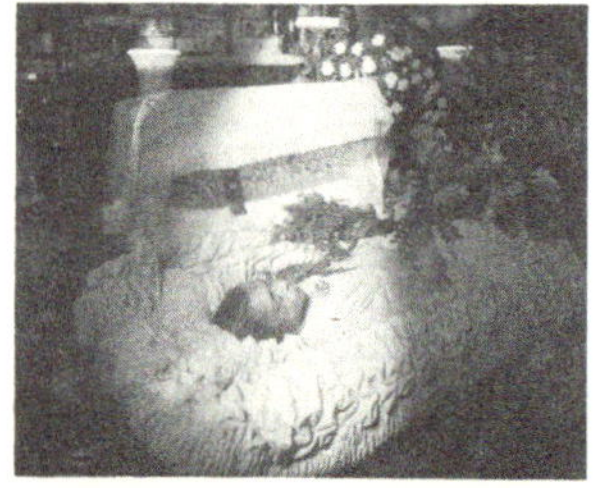

She was the mother of a man who was secretary to A. Philip Randolph. This photograph was taken in Toppins' Mortuary, which was on the same block as Micky's Funeral Home.

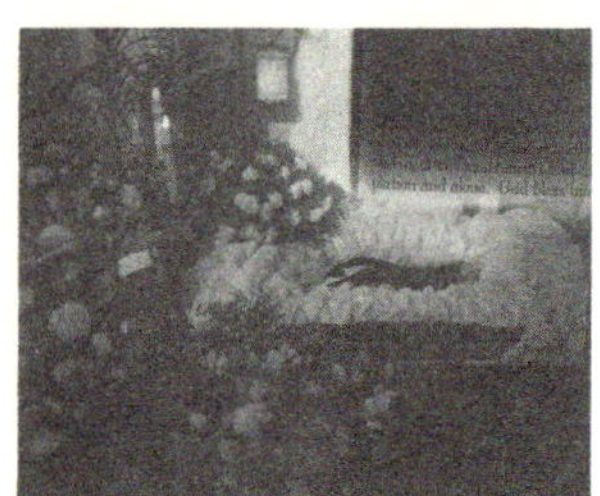

I also made pictures for some white people in the neighborhood. It was somebody's father, but don't ask me who they were 'cause I can't remember. This could have been made downtown. They might have known me because they probably had business in Harlem.

DID THE FAMILY ASK FOR ANY SPECIFIC POEM?

No, they didn't ask for nothing like that; it's just that this was their father and I put something in the picture that was appropriate for father.

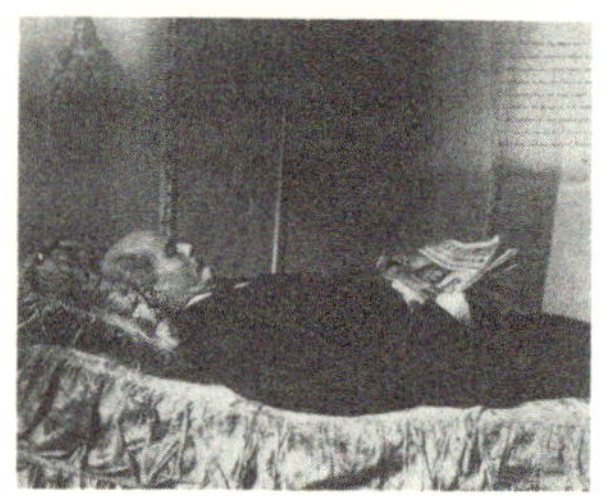

To make this dead gentleman look more natural, his family wanted the paper put in his hand, to make it appear he had been reading and had just dozed off. The headline about the death of Florence Mills was in a New York paper.

HOW DID THIS MAN DIE?

I don't know. Short of breath, I guess.

WHY DID YOU PLACE SUCH A LARGE INSERT INTO THIS PICTURE?

I thought it most appropriate for that one because it was just a small child and there wasn't many flowers, and in order to fill it up I put that particular insert in there. As I see it now, this photograph is a little unusual.

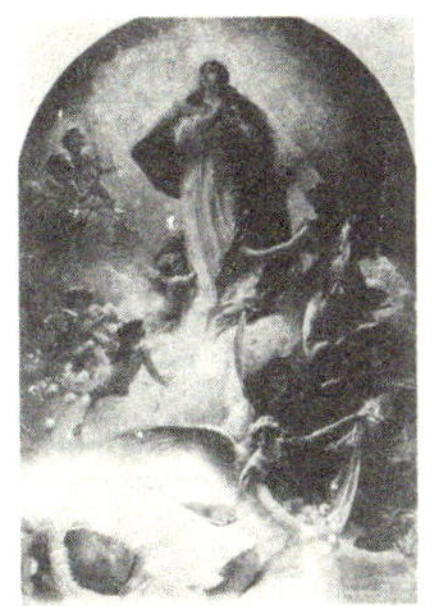

DID YOU USE DIFFERENT INSERTS FOR THE CHILDREN?

Well, it depended upon how much space I had on the picture and what the occasion was and how old the child was. In some of them I even used to color up the flowers.

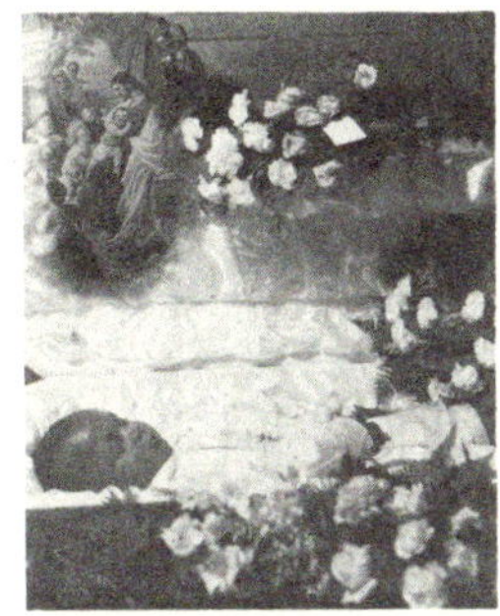

WHY WAS THE CHILD PHOTOGRAPHED IN A CRIB?

I decided to pose the child like that. The mother had wanted the child to sleep in the crib, but she had never thought she was old enough to put her in there; so she was always keeping it until she got to be a certain age. In the meantime, the child died of pneumonia. Once in a while a child died of whooping cough. I know another child who died in her sleep. She couldn't turn over, so she strangled on her own vomit; and that was one who belonged to a nurse, too.

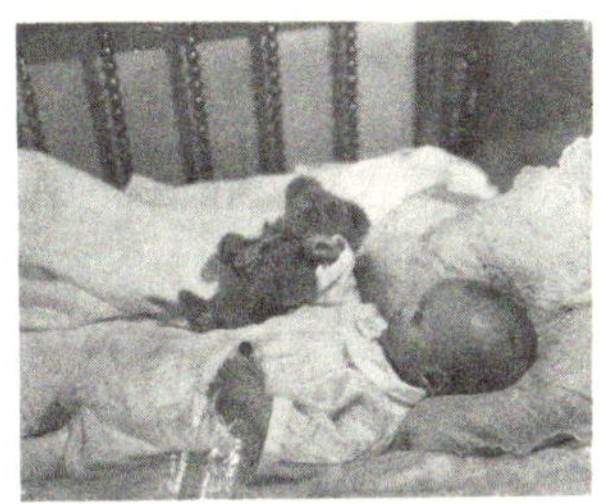

The reason for having the father hold the child was that the mother was sick in the hospital and couldn't get out. The child died in the meantime. If it wasn't for the picture, the mother wouldn't have seen the child for the last time.

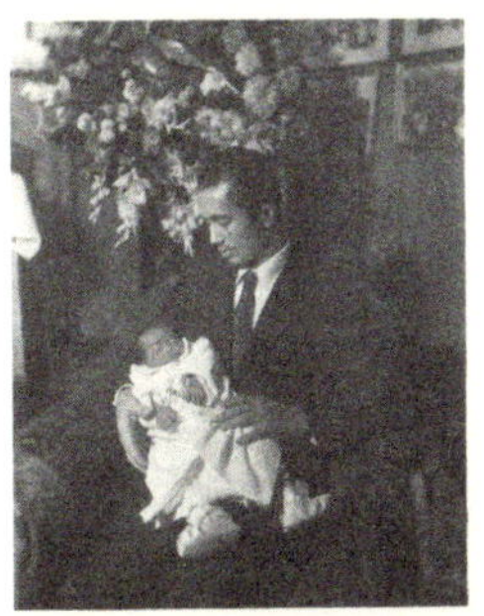

WAS THAT PICTURE TAKEN IN THEIR HOME?

No, it was taken in the funeral parlor. The radio was in the picture to make it look more homelike. It belonged to the undertaker anyway. It was my suggestion to have them hold the child while the picture was being taken to make it look more natural.

HOW DID THEY FEEL ABOUT HOLDING A DEAD CHILD?

Well it was their baby, they never had any objections. Most of these babies they all died of pneumonia; chest gets filled up with colds because they were living in cold flats. It was a very common thing in those days for people to be without heat.

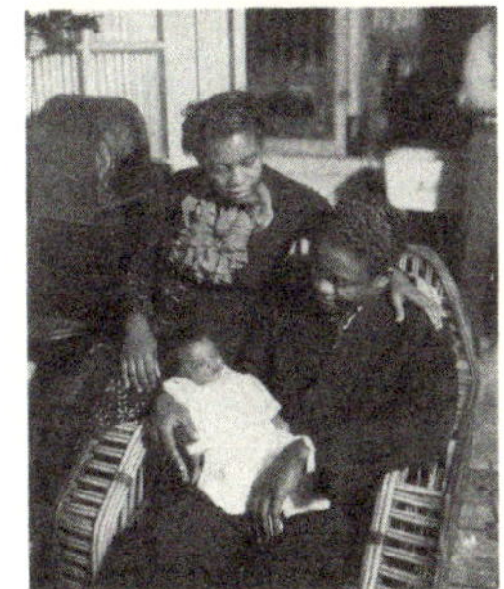

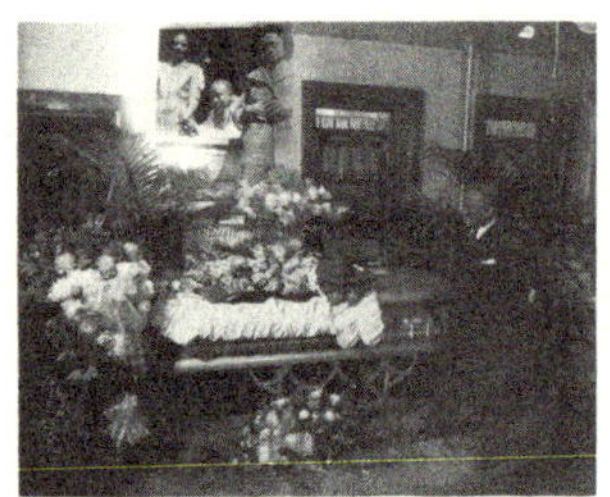

The man standing there was the father; he was very fond of that kid. As far as I know, the boy was hit by a car. He was eight or ten years old.

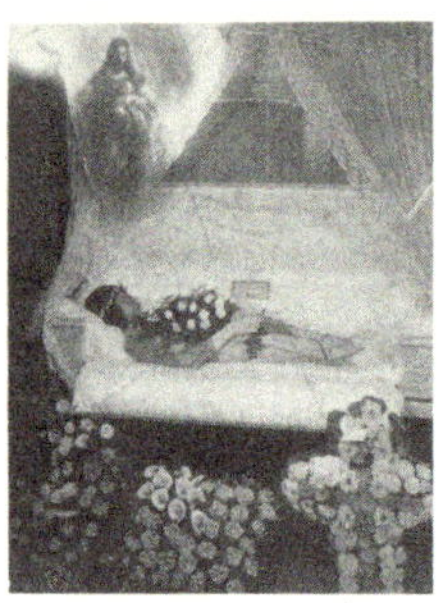

She was the one I think was shot by her sweetheart at a party with a noiseless gun. She complained of being sick at the party and friends said, "Well, why don't you lay down?" and they taken her in the room and laid her down. After they undressed her and loosened her clothes, they saw the blood on her dress. They asked her about it and she said, "I'll tell you tomorrow, yes, I'll tell you tomorrow." She was just trying to give him a chance to get away. For the picture, I placed the flowers on her chest.

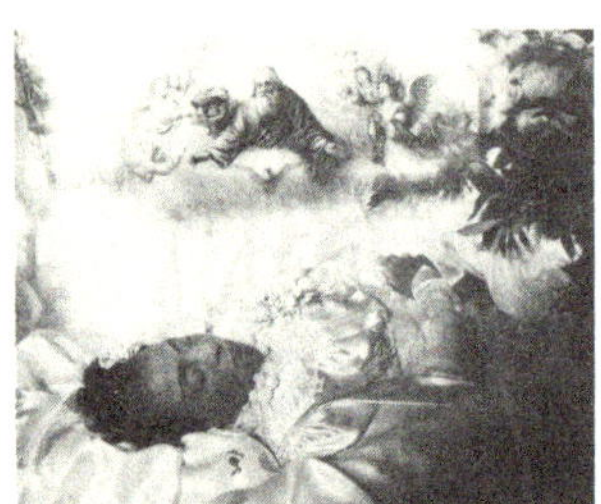

This one was at Payne's Funeral Home right across from 272 Lenox Avenue. The relatives never told me what kind of photograph they wanted, that was my decision. I always made full-length if they hadn't any flowers, and then I made a close-up after that.

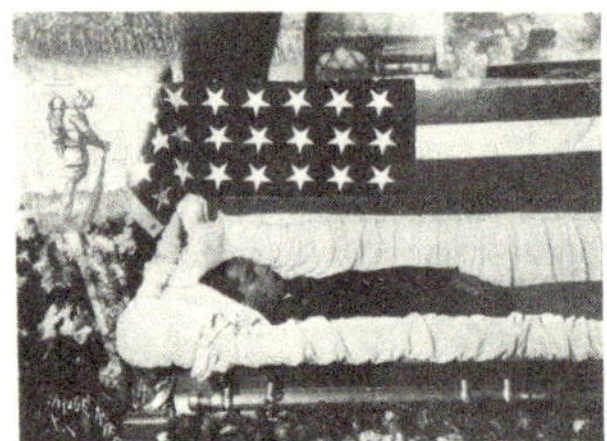

The funeral parlor supplied the flag for the military and I arranged the setting of the flowers and included the inserts, which sometimes showed the soldiers on the battlefield.

WHO WERE THESE PEOPLE?

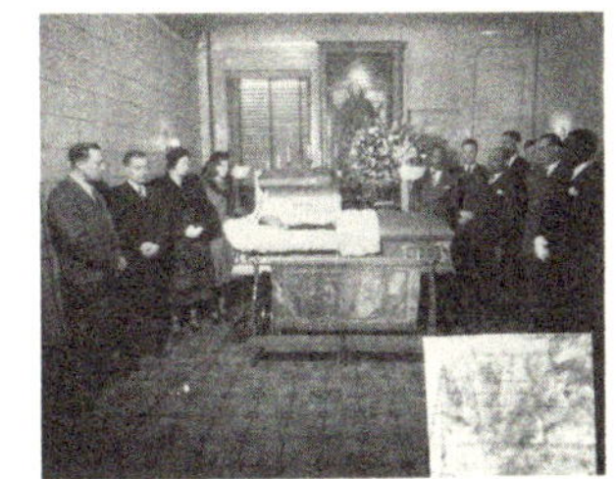

This boy used to work for the N.B.C. broadcasting company. His name was Paul; I can't think of the rest of his name. He used to live in our house. I think he stepped off the curb at 42nd St. and got hit by a car. Gaynella and I had to go down to the morgue and identify the body and make all the funeral arrangements. The people in the photograph were from the broadcasting company. I made pictures and sent them to his relatives in California. He has $2,000 in insurance. After the funerala, the money that was left was divided between the relatives in California and some he had in Boston. The photograph was taken at Undertaker Turner on 136th St. off Lenox Ave.

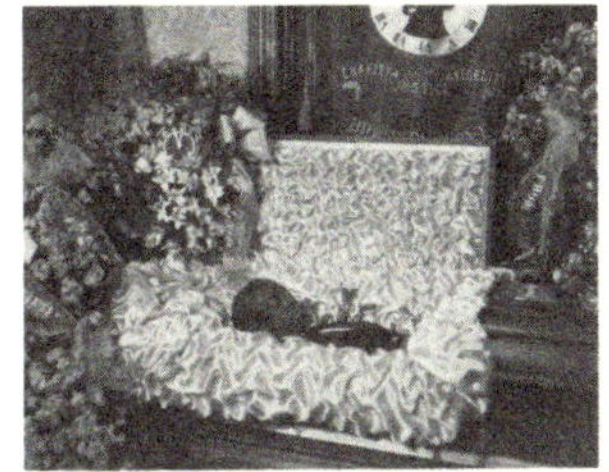

The Masonic lodges didn't call me very much, but some of the various members did.

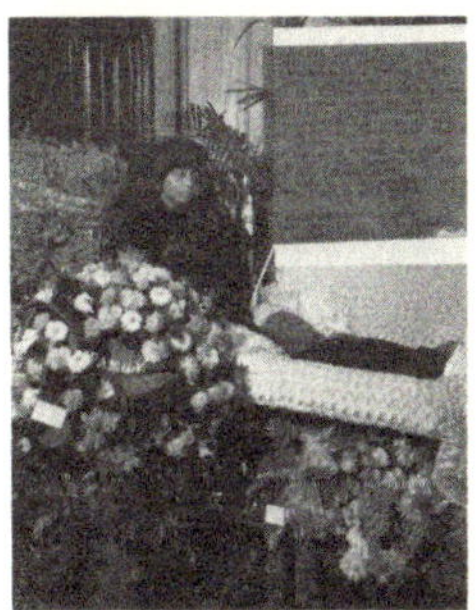

She wanted her picture taken with her husband on the day of the funeral. I don't remember her name, except that she was a taxi driver with her own cab.

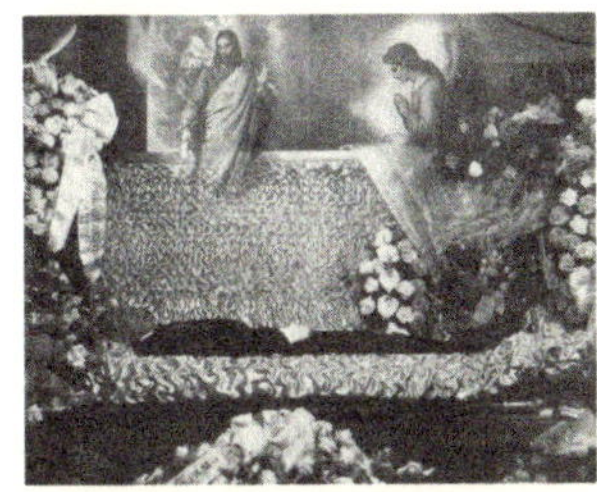

This is a very fancy casket for a man; usually they were a little more plain.

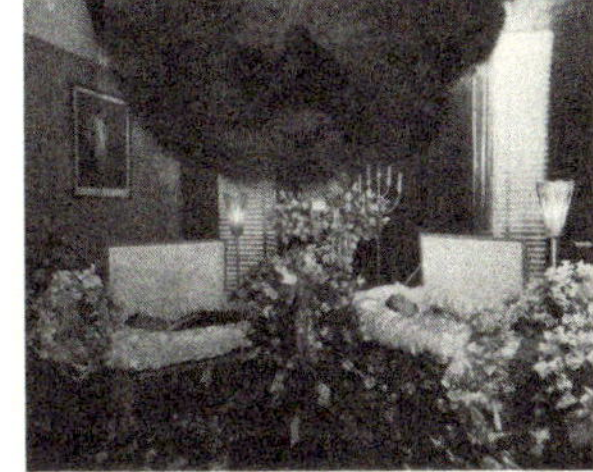

These people were brother and sister. The sister was in the hospital. In the meantime, another brother, he gets sick and dies. The brother that was out, he thought he could go to the hospital to see if he could get the sister to go to the funeral. She was only in the hospital for treatment or something. When he got there he found out that she'd been dead for a couple of days and that the hospital had been trying to locate him. Well, then he had the undertaker bring her down there to Micky's South Carolina Funeral Home where they had a double funeral. I believe it was on Lenox Avenue off 118th St.

Afterword, Afterlife

The pieces I am, she gather them and give them back to me.
Toni Morrison, *Beloved*

This now-classic collaboration between artist and sculptor Camille Billops, scholar and poet Owen Dodson, and photographer James Van Der Zee, as curious when it was first published as it is prescient today, considers the histories of African America as entwined in stories of death and dying. Although individual images from Van Der Zee's photographic archive may easily come to mind, the thematic congregation here is unique.

The Harlem Book of the Dead not only fully claimed twentieth-century Harlem as its origin story, but also institutionalized that story. Billops selected and organized Dodson's and Van Der Zee's cooperative work and then framed it within a critical textual thread: her priceless conversational interview with Van Der Zee. Dodson's poetry is a quieter accompaniment, notable as much for the visual space it claims in the composition of the book as for the way that his meticulous reading of the photographic subject is rendered into verse. But Van Der Zee's extraordinary images are what finally locate this community and assign it the particularity of Harlem as the site of its creation—a decision that gave requisite and full acknowledgment to Black America's most globally recognized homeplace. And, despite these artists' collaboration, photography is its voice. Van Der Zee is speaker for the dead.

This book was imagined, composed, and then bound, bordered, and crafted by Billops. It gained a certain animation in Dodson's poetry, but Billops's intelligent and visionary culling through Van Der Zee's oeuvre brought the project into the sensory project that would become a classic publication in American arts and letters. Although a few of the artist's mortuary photographs had been published before (albeit without acknowledgment that these were works by James Van Der Zee),[1] this is the only published project that focused solely on his photographs of the dead. These images secured the souls of Harlem's Black folk.

In "A Very Long Conversation with James Van Der Zee at the Age of Ninety-One," an interview that weaves throughout the text, Billops's prodding and the artist's fulsome responses help readers appreciate how the selected photographs for this text were culled from a voluminous, arguably overwhelming archive. By focusing on Van Der Zee's mortuary photography, giving the images order and context, and then placing Dodson's sometimes-florid poems alongside them as accompaniment, Billops fashioned the portraits into a narrative that could testify to the claim of "Harlem" in the title. These stilled lives have an afterlife because of this collaboration between the artist, the poet, and the photographer.

Despite the book's seductive title, Van Der Zee's Harlem is no site of mourning. Instead, *The Harlem Book of the Dead* accomplishes the work one finds in a funeral program's reserved and necessary space for the obituary. Like that historic and cultural programmatic placeholder, this book's voices, images, and texts fashion an exquisitely constructed memory. It offers an afterlife not unlike the ritual of the obituary, where a biography, customarily printed alongside the order of service, ensures that a family, a congregation of mourners, and generations beyond are able to pass on the lives of Harlem's folk.

Section chapters gather these Harlem communities: "Mothers & Prophecies," "Fathers & the Better People," "Women: Wives & Friends," and "Mourners & the Posing of the Dead." The configurations within these gatherings, where the living claim a space in the stories—within the photographic plates, or as onlookers or readers—returns the photographic subjects back to the vigor that circumstance has buried. The sounds, sensations, and legendary scenes of Harlem collaborate here.

When I speak to audiences about these images, I often have to direct viewers to notice the sometimes subtle artistry in their deliberate composition. Certainly, the dramatic overlay of lyrics and poetry, flags, religious iconography, or floral cascades that edge and sometimes spill from the caskets and even the frames of the images can be flamboyant. The interview between Van Der Zee and Billops explains some of these decisions, recounting how he chose the overlays for a particular emphasis or perspective. As a practice, Van Der Zee's aesthetic composed a cultivated vision of an afterlife, a stilled life, as well as one that might encourage a momentary but pregnant pause in the practiced ritual of the Black funeral. A simple photograph, the Kodak or Polaroid photo a family member might take and add to a scrapbook, could certainly be a reminder of the moment and the body. The *excess* of life and art that fills these photographs is artifact. For example, on page 37, a photograph in the section "Children & the Mystery of Birth" assures the reader that Harlem's babies were born, loved, and lingered over. In this image, Van Der Zee arranges a storied life, turning the funeral home's parlor into a "living" room where the parents hold the body of their child and lovingly fix their gaze on their babe. But some viewers may not notice the almost ghostly figure of the mortician in the top right corner. Although Van Der Zee could easily have cropped the mortician from the image, he preserved the figure in order to acknowledge that a full story lies within the frame. The mortician is a shadowy, stalwart presence nearly fading into the background and standing watch, ready to remove the baby's body from the father's grasp and place the infant back into the casket. An even more careful look into the background of this image reveals a child-sized casket—a slightly blurred, white-flocked vessel positioned just behind the undertaker. Van Der Zee's artistry depends on dimensionality and commands our intimate viewing. The photographer paused the business of burial to construct our reflection on mourning and memory.

The text accomplishes this task as well. Side-by-side notations that Billops titled "Description of Plates" follow Dodson's final décima, "The Pastor." This section is best read as a complement to the preacher's close of the text, making certain that the last word is both visual and textual. The "Description of Plates" is a glossary of Van Der Zee's deliberative practice. It is here that he explains how the image referenced above was actually taken in the funeral parlor—an establishment that clearly trafficked in the place-names of home—and reveals how he arranged the scene to look "homelike" by placing a radio in the frame. The exquisite practice of his art lay in his gathering up of the lives, deaths, and ephemera of Harlem's communities.

Although the intentional allusion to iconic Egyptian Book of the Dead might first claim our attention, and even though this is an important reference for the project, Van Der Zee's photographs echo the traditions of memento mori photographic artistry from the Victorian era.[2] Indeed, in placing Black folk into the high art of that European aesthetic tradition, Van Der Zee claims the Black body as a grievable subject, one worthy of an artist's gaze and a community's memory. Just as a funeral program is carefully kept, stored like family treasure, gathered up (sometimes bound with a black silk ribbon), and carefully preserved in a bureau drawer, piano bench, or family scrapbook, this book gathers Harlem.

Camille Billops clearly places Harlem into a space shared with royal funeral traditions when she writes in her introduction that "Harlem rituals have parallels with those of the ancient necropolis of Egypt." The title's gesture to Egypt, first suggested in the typeface and the Egyptian/Art Deco aesthetic of its cover art, engages the dreamscape of a Harlem generation for whom Northern Africa (Ethiopia and Egypt in particular) held a certain resonance with Black arts.

As a scholar and teacher, Owen Dodson cultivated a professional life framed by the final waves of the Harlem Renaissance. The tension between Dodson's classical training and the language and styles practiced by Harlem Renaissance poets is beautifully held in lines that match traditional poetic forms and display Harlem's vernacular. Some fully incorporate the abbreviated lines as well as first-person voices of the Renaissance poets: "This casket's right pretty / Satin everywhere." And others, like the elegiac "Allegory of Seafaring Black Mothers," claim classical motifs to tell a Black story. Dodson's word-work testifies to the complex textures of this book.

Despite the way that the construction of *The Harlem Book of the Dead* encourages its unfolding alongside Dodson's accompanying poetic text, Van Der Zee's voice makes up the album's liner notes. "A Very Long Conversation" is an expository, narratively inclined interlude that reads more like an interview than a conversational exchange between Billops and the photographer. Its prominence in the text, weaving between photographs and poetry, is critical and strategic.

Although the array of textual sites, voice, and image offers up a collective and congregational voice for Harlem's dead, the text finally comes to rest with James Van Der Zee's images. His provocative, curious, and introspective photographs of Harlem's folks have the final say. This is an open casket viewing. This is what it means to compose an afterlife.

Karla FC Holloway

1. See Cecil Beaton, *Cecil Beaton's New York* (B. T. Batsford, 1938; repr., Forgotten Books, 2018). The subtitle of this book, *Illustrated From Drawings by the Author and From Photographs by the Author and Others*, suggests that Beaton's failure to name Van Der Zee was an intentional oversight that "other" artists included in Beaton's view of New York also experienced. No one but Beaton was associated with their illustrations or photographs. It was an unfortunate slight.

2. See Karla FC Holloway, *Passed On: African American Mourning Stories; A Memorial* (Duke University Press, 2002). "African Americans upheld the tradition of formal portraiture of the dead in final sleep, a tradition Euro-America did not continue into the twentieth century. . . . [D]omestic artistry of photographic composition, with [its] deliberate framing of the effects of home and hearth within the image, argued the cultural familiarity of black death" (27, 30).

The Harlem Book of the Dead

ISBN 979-8-9910367-2-6

Editor (1978): Camille Billops
Designer (1978): John O'Mara
Managing Editors (2025): Garrett Bradley and James Hoff
Designer (2025): Bryce Wilner
Copy Editor (2025): Allison Dubinsky

Primary Information
232 3rd Street, #A113
Brooklyn, NY 11215
www.primaryinformation.org

Printed by Grafiche Veneziane, Italy

Primary Information and Garrett Bradley would like to thank Hilton Als, Connie H. Choi, Gabrielle M. Dudley, Thelma Golden, Ryan Haley, Yelena Keller, Sing Lee Nathan, Karan Rinaldo, Jeff Rosenheim, Legacy Russell, and Candice Yates.

The Metropolitan Museum of Art is pleased to collaborate with Primary Information and Garrett Bradley to publish this facsimile edition of James Van Der Zee's previously out-of-print book, *The Harlem Book of the Dead*, and place this influential work in the hands of a contemporary audience.

In December 2021, The Met established the James Van Der Zee Archive, in partnership with the Studio Museum in Harlem. The objective is to research, conserve, and provide full public access to the remarkable archive of photographer James Van Der Zee (1886–1983). Van Der Zee was one of the most celebrated chroniclers of Black life in New York City during the Harlem Renaissance, and for decades thereafter. The Archive represents the largest public collection of the artist's work and comprises approximately 20,000 lifetime prints, 30,000 negatives, studio equipment, business records, and ephemera. With this acquisition came the responsibility of administering copyright for works created by James Van Der Zee and serving as caretaker of this important artist's legacy.

Department of Photographs
The Metropolitan Museum of Art